C000152568

RENAISSANCE MAN:
The Lin-Manuel Miranda Story
An Unauthorized Biography

NY Times Best-seller
MARC SHAPIRO

For more information contact:
Riverdale Avenue Books
5676 Riverdale Avenue
Riverdale, NY 10471.

www.riverdaleavebooks.com

Design by www.formatting4U.com
Cover by Scott Carpenter

Digital ISBN: 978-1-62601-449-7

Print ISBN: 978-1-62601-448-0

First Edition May, 2018

Dedication:

This book is dedicated to my father, Bennie Shapiro, who was born in Lithuania and came to this country at a young age. He joined the army during World War II, was stationed in Germany and was MIA for ten days before being found. He married and had three kids, of which I was the oldest. He worked in the Los Angeles Garment District. He was a great husband and a great father. He was a straightforward, no bullshit blue-collar guy who loved his weekly poker games. The highlight of his week was when he took us to a deli in Boyle Heights for lox and bagels. He was always reading the newspaper. He took me to my very first horror film. He convinced me not to smoke at age six when he stuck a lighted cigarette in my mouth and said, "inhale." He told me he would support me in anything that I wanted to do with my life, but if I did the same thing he did he would kick my ass. When I got kicked out of junior high school for fighting, I figured I would catch holy hell from him so I called him at work to tell him the bad news. All he wanted to know was whether I fought back. When I said yes, he said that was all he needed to know. My father died suddenly at age 40. He was gone way too soon. I miss him every day.

Table of Contents

Author's Notes
How His Mind Works

I read the papers. Consequently, I knew a lot about the Broadway smash *Hamilton* and how it was the brainchild of Lin-Manuel Miranda, the new kid on the Broadway block. But I was observing from afar. I had yet to see *Hamilton* and thus, was forming my opinions much in the way most casual observers do, by the regularly laudatory and often fawning entertainment press. My gut told me that there was something there. Something beyond the glitz, glamour and hype.

Ultimately, it would take my five year-old granddaughter Lily to set me on the right track.

Like most five year olds, Lily has been quick to obsess with all things *Moana*. I've lost track of how many times she's watched the movie and it seems like every time she's at our house or in our car, the soundtrack is playing, loud and clear, on a seemingly constant loop. And through a combination of sheer repetition and the inherent, bouncy catchiness of the music, much of which was written by Miranda, I started to get the hint.

There is a whole lot to like in Miranda, a whole lot of bubbly and positive, a whole lot of spot on. Miranda's approach to creation is a very potent mix.

There will be time for all the deep thinking and examination later. But for now, let's just say it like it is.

Miranda is a pop culture mix-master of ideas, thought and passion. Somebody who can take our hopes and dreams and send them back to us wrapped in a bright musical bow.

Growing up, everything in Miranda's world resonated with possibility. The years listening to his parent's massive record collection, the countless hours spent in dark movie houses feeding off the latest Disney fantasies like *The Little Mermaid*, his mania for theatrical music, the live fire of theater and his immediate attraction to the lyrical power of hip hop music. Miranda took it all in and creatively spit it back out. He is like most of us who take our youthful fascinations and hope to somehow, some way make a life of it. The only difference being that Lin-Manuel Miranda did it. He's taken everything from *Jesus Christ Superstar* and *West Side Story* to the latest beats from the street and turned them from passion to life as the two creative drives crossed paths on the road to greatness.

Miranda as the world-wide, much-celebrated creative force, is quite simply a creature of his influences, observations and the simplicity of the world around him. There is savvy and a gut level sense of knowledge in every bit of music and every lyric he creates, and let's not forget a very traditional sense of right and wrong, which he has in spades. His plays and music like *Hamilton*, *In the Heights* and *Bring It On: The Musical*, as well as his contributions to the soundtrack of the movie *Moana* and even his bit of fun in *Star Wars: The Force Awakens*, are like fruit from a creative tree. In Miranda's mind, even the most simple of moments are fodder for creative thought and interpretation how Miranda goes about his business is not that difficult to figure out. Quite simply, he sees his world as ripe with possibilities and he takes advantage of them on a daily basis.

Miranda is so tuned in to ideas around him that it is not surprising that even his memories and casual observations of everyday life burst with flights of fancy and a sense of lilt and storytelling depth. He has a keen eye for where he comes from, where he's been and, perhaps most importantly, where he's going.

Miranda was also entrenched in seemingly endless layers of influence, growing up in a world of show tunes, hip hop, rap, pop and a myriad of other musical styles. It is the security blanket he returns to quite often, refining and infusing traditional notions with the possibilities of a future wrapped up in the new and different.

That Lin-Manuel Miranda has emerged as the pop composer/literal renaissance man of his time was the logical reason to profile his life. *Hamilton* is on everybody's lips and so, in the immortal words of the publishing bard, strike while the iron is hot became the order of the day. But it soon became something a bit more than cashing in on the latest big thing.

There was a classic story to be told here on a seemingly grand scale. Miranda was a young man of obvious talent, navigating an often surreal landscape full of creative possibilities and choices. The odds seemed forever in his favor no matter the obstacles. His story was never less than interesting, often bordering on the unbelievable and the just plain lucky. He was also a principled character with nary a hint of scandal or TMZ gossip to mar the odyssey. Quite simply, Lin-Manuel Miranda was just too busy being himself to indulge in any questionable behavior.

And trust me, the question of such good behavior struck me as occasionally "how could that be?" After all, Miranda was a literal babe in the woods, in the best possible way often childlike, whose passions and goals put him in direct conflict with the often unfair and unscrupulous world of entertainment. I was convinced that there had to be a bump in the road somewhere. I looked but found nothing. He was just a good guy going about his business being a creative spirit.

Truth be told, the life story of Lin-Manuel Miranda would make one hell of a Broadway musical. Are you listening Lin-Manuel?

So it was with the goal of creating a definitive biography, sometimes highbrow and always creatively challenging the norm, that my publisher and I set about formulating the proper framework for this book. From the word go, we tweaked and fine-tuned the important elements to explore Miranda's life but ultimately agreed on the direction.

Hitting the high points was easy. *Hamilton*, *Moana*, *In the Heights* and *Bring It On: The Musical*, would all be major components. But what would ultimately prove the guiding light in Miranda's tale would be the seemingly small moments within those larger than life triumphs and the many minor characters and associates that would filter in and out of Miranda's life, offering guidance, influence and, often, just plain laughs to a story that never seemed to stray far from joyous.

So channeling Miranda and his world, I would be off and running.

And there would be a lot of moments to choose from. Research brought heretofore unknown names and moments at every turn. The life of a true creative personality is never far from another enticing anecdote and even the minutia was never less than enticing. In his travels, Miranda mixed with a lot of interesting people in their own right and tracking them down would be a challenge all its own.

Email requests and interview queries flew; often meeting with polite rejections or just plain ignored requests. I had long ago gotten used to idea of people not wanting to talk about a famous person they knew back in the day. And so I was most delighted when somebody, a former schoolteacher, agreed to an interview. On the other side of the coin, another former teacher agreed to an interview but when she contacted Miranda and he said he knew nothing about this book, she politely backed out.

One thing I discovered early in the process was that Lin-Manuel Miranda's life was fairly straightforward in its telling. He was born, then he did this, then he did that and, slowly but surely, his drive and talent morphed into what he has become today; success and a happy ending. However, what made this telling so damned exciting and constantly interesting was the proverbial meat on the bones, the moments in between the moments, the flash and the fantasy between the chiseled in stone 'facts.'

All the biographies I have written 'til this point have had some level of attraction for me, otherwise they would not have been worth doing, so I am proud to add *Renaissance Man: The Lin-Manuel Miranda Story* to that list. There is energy and excitement at every turn. There is the ever-present chance of creative life and possibility at the turn of the page.

Renaissance Man: The Lin-Manuel Miranda Story is a book I would read if I had not already had a front row seat to its creation, because it would have been just too damned interesting to pass up.

Marc Shapiro
April 2018

Introduction
Now It's Time to Say Goodbye

"God! What have I done?"

For Lin-Manuel Miranda, the not-too-subtle turn of phrase uttered to *The Guardian* was more than mere exclamation or the obvious footnote to a job well down. For the creator and star of *Hamilton*, it was trademark Miranda, equal parts youthful triumph and the verbal equivalent of winning a gold medal and crossing the finish line. *Hamilton* had made both Miranda's career and his legacy as a driving force in theater.

And, as of July 2016, that aspect of his career was about to close. Because it was on a night at the Richard Rodgers Theater in New York, that Miranda took a final curtain call and bow, effectively bringing his tenure as the hip hop Hamilton to a close after what had been a record setting year-long run on Broadway.

And, perhaps most importantly, *Hamilton* had reportedly given the Broadway theater community a long anticipated shot in the arm. Not that the Great White Way was in a creative valley, far from it. Theaters were regularly packed and the quality was high. But the fare was safe, old warhorses being trotted out with a fresh rider and plays cobbled together from hit films. At the end of the day, what was missing was the daring, the adventure, the willingness to take a chance. Enter *Hamilton*.

During the run of the historical musical, *Hamilton* had sold one billion dollars in tickets, had captured a Pulitzer Prize and was honored with 11 Tony Awards. *Hamilton* was a groundbreaking effort in the realm of modern musical theater and, the literal hipness and cool of this ultra- modern telling of one of America's most underappreciated founding fathers, made *Hamilton* a magnet that regularly drew celebrities as divergent as Busta Rhymes, Mandy Patinkin, Prince, Lenny Kravitz and Lee Daniels. But for two hours and 45 minutes each night, for eight shows a week, the focus was on Miranda, an only marginally successful composer/actor in the Broadway theater world up to that point, who held court at center stage as the mercurial, electrifying modern-day reincarnation of Hamilton, whose life and times were brought to the stage amid a wealth of passionate dance moves and world rhythms.

But it was safe to say that Miranda, after finishing up what many would conclude was a theatrical marathon of massive proportions, did not appear to be much the worse for wear. He appeared a very boyish looking 36, and with his slight frame, sly smile and a telling sense of humor and irony that often made him appear simultaneously a seasoned adult and a precocious, confident teen.

These sides of Miranda were alternately on display at the conclusion of his stint in *Hamilton* when he willingly engaged in a series of wrap-up interviews, in various places in and around New York's Broadway as well as the odd nostalgic turn conducted in Washington Heights, the Manhattan neighborhood where he grew up. The overriding message during those interviews was that, yes, Miranda was, for the foreseeable future, through with *Hamilton* as an on-stage presence and that, equally forthright, it was the right time to go.

"I was ready," he acknowledged in a conversation with *Gentleman's Quarterly*. "My kid (a boy named Sebastian) was born two weeks before rehearsals for *Hamilton* started. By the time I finished up with *Hamilton* he was starting to speak in complete sentences. I leave *Hamilton* very tired and very fulfilled. But I also have enough stuff going on in real life that I didn't need *Hamilton* to be the rest of my life."

And while Miranda was anxious to start on the next phase of his by now burgeoning professional career, which meant putting the final touches on his songs for the soundtrack of *Moana* and flying off to London to act in the buzz-worthy and long anticipated *Mary Poppins Returns*. There is also a busman's holiday of sorts in which Miranda will be putting together an homage to his roots with a star-studded mixtape with a growing list of hip hop and rap contributors. But through it all, Miranda makes it plain that his short-term goal was to get back into what he considers "the real world" of being a family man with his wife Vanessa and his son Sebastian and to put friends before career whenever it was humanly possible.

"I found out that Prince was going to be in the audience for a performance of *Hamilton*," Miranda remembered in an interview with *Gentleman's Quarterly*. "It turned out that one of my best friends was getting married that same day. I had promised him that I would be there for the wedding and at the end of the day that was more important than looking out into the audience and seeing Prince."

He further chuckled in the same *GQ* interview that, these days, he is spending a lot of time picking up dog poop and changing his son's diapers. "I learned early on that having success does not get you out of life."

But as he contemplates life post-*Hamilton*, Miranda is nothing if not humbled by his rags to riches rise and ultimately philosophical about the past and the future. "I went from being a broke substitute teacher to a Broadway composer," he said in an interview with *National Public Radio* as the enormity of his life's journey to that point and what the future would most certainly bring was beginning to sink in." I will never make a leap that big in my life again."

Miranda smiled that smile that teases and warns that even when literally and figuratively sitting on top of the world, nothing is really ever over. "When it comes to *Hamilton*, I don't think I'm remotely done with it."

Chapter One
Once Upon a Time in America

There was a lot in the life and times of Alexander Hamilton that would seem to foreshadow what would, most certainly, light a fire under Miranda more than a century later.

For openers, Hamilton, an acknowledged founding father of the fledgling United States of America, was not born in America but rather, the British West Indies. To add further intrigue to Hamilton's story, Hamilton was born out of wedlock to a Scottish man and a married woman named Rachel Faucette. And finally, there was the long-standing speculation, often cited over the years and, most recently, in author Ron Chernow's excellent best-selling biography *Alexander Hamilton*, that Hamilton's mother was of half British and half French Huguenot descent and that Hamilton was, in fact, of mixed race.

Stories like these have tantalized historians for countless decades. But it would take genealogist Megan Smolenyak a period of sheer admiration for Miranda and his work to set her on the path to discovering his true roots. Smolenyak, who is noted for having traced the respective family trees of Barack and Michelle Obama, Joe Biden and Prince, and who serves as a consultant for the American television series *Who Do You Think You Are?* acknowledged in a blog entry that was ultimately excerpted by *The Guardian*, "I had become a fan of the *Hamilton* soundtrack. Every once in a while, out of plain respect and admiration, I decide to research someone."

Early aspects of the research on Miranda's family tree focused on the early 1800's where two bits of history immediately presented themselves. On July 11, 1804, Alexander Hamilton died in a pistol duel against long time foe Aaron Burr. The second bit of history, a bit more obscure, would touch a lot closer to home.

After nearly a month of research, Smolenyak eventually discovered what she believed was ground zero for Lin-Manuel Miranda's family tree in the guise of an interracial couple named David and Sophie Towns. They were as her research indicated, the great, great, great, great, great grandparents of Miranda.

David was a white southerner from North Carolina who met and married Sophie, a formerly black slave from Virginia after a tumultuous period in his life which included the death of both parents and a first wife, a decade removed from the infamous Hamilton/Burr duel. While interracial relationships were not unusual at the time, when the final outcome of the Civil War had only put a mild dent in the notion of laws regarding the freedom of slaves and, most importantly for David and Sophie, the rights and legalities of interracial relationships and marriage.

The couple, whose marriage has been loosely pegged at 1811, immediately ran afoul of the state of Virginia, which did not tolerate anything approaching equal status for freed slaves and interracial marriage.

Seeing themselves held back politically and socially in Virginia, David and Sophie moved to a much more tolerant Louisiana in 1815 and welcomed the first of what would ultimately be at least nine children (records on such matters were far from airtight at that time). The couple would thrive in Louisiana until 1826 when David, Sophie and their by then six children relocated to what was shaping up as the new post-Civil War level of tolerance in the city of Nacogdoches, in the recently named country of Mexico where immigrants of any race, color and nationality were welcomed with open arms and the freedom of post Civil War slaves and their children was honored.

For his part, David was active on the US political front, lobbying for legislation that would eventually result in landmark laws supporting recognized freedom for slaves and former slaves and a growing tolerance for mixed race marriages. Sophie died in 1838 but by that time, the Towns family had spread their family tree throughout Mexico and into parts of Texas where the ensuing generations propagated through mixed-race marriages, primarily through marriages to Mexicans and those of Mexican heritage, but also of note being the couple's first born son John marrying former slave Mary Anne Smith.

Although Smolenyak's research resulted in more than its share of conjecture, including the question of to what degree the Towns family spread into Puerto Rico, the genealogist was convinced that there was evidence that indicated certainty on the subject. "If you think about it," she said in *The Guardian* excerpt of her blog chronicling the research, "this portion of Lin-Manuel Miranda's family was multiracial, multicultural and multinational. In short, they have a lot in common with his Puerto Rican forebears."

Smolenyak was so excited about what she was discovering that she fired off a detailed tweet to Miranda. "I tweeted the thing and darned if he didn't respond to me," she related in *The Guardian*. It was beyond generous of him."

Miranda's response was understated, to say the least. "My mom's side of the family has a history as complicated as our country itself."

Miranda's comment was not merely tossed off. If nothing else, Luz Towns Miranda's mother's mere birth indicates that the Towns family did, indeed, make its way to Puerto Rico. As noted in *My Heritage.com*, Miranda's mother, Luz Towns, was born in Puerto Rico to Pedro, a Mexican American father and Pascal Towns, a Puerto Rican mother. The Towns family quickly saw the opportunity for a better life and would move to the United States when Luz was a young child.

From the outset, Luz Towns was considered a bright and curious child, one who saw the big picture. As she grew from childhood to adult with the constant encouragement of her parents, was always on a higher educational path and the knowledge it would bring. especially as it would pertain to the mental health of the family and, in particular, children and the reality of birth control.

"In my junior year at an all-girls Catholic high school, one of my classmates went on spring vacation and never came back," Miranda recalled in a conversation with *Vogue*. "Such disappearances, which were provoked by unexpected pregnancies, were not uncommon."

Luz, wise beyond her years, was well aware that a lack of contraceptive programs in Puerto Rico often resulted in forced marriages, illegal abortions and the inevitable cutting short the potential of young women's lives. All of which turned Miranda in the direction of a career that would medically and psychologically help young women and families deal with these challenges, both societal and personal. Shortly after finishing her formal education, Towns traveled to New York where she would cut her teeth on various psychological jobs while continuing to further her Masters' degree program in psychology at New York University.

It was there that she met Luis A. Miranda Jr., also from Puerto Rico, who was on an odyssey of his own.

Miranda Jr., born in Vega Alta Puerto Rico on August 23, 1954, was, like Towns, a very self directed and committed child. Extremely bookish and education driven, Miranda Jr. was a seeker at a very young age. Miranda Jr. was very much a product of his familial environment. Everybody in his family seemed to have been cut from varying degrees of entrepreneurial cloth. Miranda Jr. recalled as much in an interview with *NBC News.* "My mother owned the travel agency in town and my sister owned the school supply store."

And as stories were often passed down within a family from father and son, years later Lin-Manuel Miranda, in a speech before The Broadway League, would disclose, seemingly for the first time in a public arena that his interest in the creative arts may well have had his genetic roots in his father's early upbringing.

"My father's uncle, Ernesto Concepcion, was the

founder of the Actor's Guild of Puerto Rico. His first memories were of his uncle playing the role of John Merrick in *The Elephant Man*. One minute he is kissing his uncle hello backstage and the next he is seeing his uncle as John Merrick in a room full of crying people. He sees the man in front of him as both his uncle and not his uncle and nothing is ever really the same again."

But as he would disclose in the same The Broadway League speech, his father's emotional and spiritual coming of age would be in 1961 when, at age seven he attended a screening of *West Side Story* in the only movie house in Vega Alta. "There is that moment where Maria is standing over Tony, and Schrank and Krupke are going to pick up the body. Maria screams 'Don't you touch him!' and the audience laughs. But my father is in tears. He is seven years old and he is balling."

At that formative age, Luis immediately discovered the yin and yang of live theater and the movies and the differing emotions it can bring. Miranda recalled that it would be an important turning point in his life. "This was my father's moment of action. He looked around at everyone laughing at the grieving Puerto Rican widow and he said 'I've got to get the fuck out of this town.'"

Miranda Jr. was driven by the world around him and soon found himself gravitating toward the real world machinations and ramifications of Puerto Rican politics. The consequences of political and social actions within his country fascinated him, as did the process by which political action could influence change. Considered by many to be a child prodigy, Miranda Jr. was always well ahead of his grade level and would enter and complete graduation in a top Puerto Rican university well before his 18th birthday.

Miranda Jr. was driven and soon restless in his quest for knowledge. What he had learned in Puerto Rico was most certainly just a taste of what was out there. At a young age, he was seemingly headed for a life and career in any of a number of upper class, white collar occupations in his home country. But he was young enough and curious enough that he was soon attracted to the possibility of travelling to the United States and increasing his sense of the world. Luis was on the cusp of a very difficult decision as he would relate years later in a conversation with *GQ*.

"When I was 18, I gave up a very safe job as the manager of the biggest Sears department store in Puerto Rico to go to New York and to try and get my degree. I didn't speak the language. Nothing in my life prepared me for that moment. My decision didn't make sense."

But Luis was driven, confident and fascinated by the possibilities of this great and illogical adventure. And so, shortly after he turned 18, Miranda Jr. left Puerto Rico for New York and was soon enrolled at New York University where he enrolled in a high level graduate program in Clinical Psychology.

And it would turn out to be a decision that Luis would acknowledge was totally against his normal way of dealing with life. He had a very working man way of thinking about him, a conservative attitude that equated with a hard day's work for a hard day's pay. But as he recalled in *Playbill.com*, he suddenly saw temptation over the horizon. "When I was 17, I was the manager of a Sears store in Puerto Rico and I basically threw that all away to go to New York. I didn't speak a bit of English.

Going to New York made absolutely no sense but it was what I needed to do."

Those at NYU were immediately impressed. Towns, in particular, recalled in a *New York Lifestyle* interview that when Miranda Jr. came to the U.S. "he was the youngest student ever accepted into the University's clinical psychology program."

Towns and Miranda Jr's. classroom friendship seemingly quickly turned into a romantic relationship. They were in synch in almost all ways personal and professional, had their Puerto Rican heritage in common and were driven in their creative and life attitudes. Towns was the more creatively oriented while Miranda Jr. displayed a more real world, practical and, by degrees, conservative attitude. It was the classic case of opposites attracting. Love soon blossomed into marriage in the early 70's and, by 1973, the happy couple announced that Miranda was pregnant with the couple's first child.

The ensuing months were a beehive of activity. The Miranda's were finishing up bits and pieces of their respective education. For, his part, Miranda Jr. had come to the reality that he was more inclined toward political involvement as his life's work and set about attempting to figure out how politics in America worked.

"I can't remember when I was not involved in politics," he offered to *amNY.com*. "When I arrived in America, it took me a while to find my place in the Democratic/Republican divide."

Luz Miranda was born on November 26, 1973. In the most ironic way, the Mirandas and the Towns had come full circle on their family tree and were once again laying down roots in America. Only this time they were not slaves.

Chapter Two
Welcome to Inwood

With the birth of their first child, the Mirandas set about immersing themselves into a middle class American way of life. And if the unwritten stereotype of the times held any validity, if you were various shades of brown or black and of limited means in the vicinity of New York City, that meant you most likely ended up in Northern Manhattan. And the Mirandas found themselves at the Northern-most tip of Manhattan Island in the Inwood neighborhood.

Inwood was right on the border with the more well-known and, by degrees, more affluent Washington Heights, with a view of the Harlem River to the very left and the Hudson River on the right. The neighborhood, with all its greenery, could appear both picturesque and appealing and downtrodden and somewhat crime ridden/decaying. To those who lived there, it provided a surprisingly reassuring sense of family and comfort, equal parts Harlem and *West Side Story*. For all its low key presentation, Inwood was the proving grounds of a number of future notables such as author Jim Carroll (*The Basketball Diaries*), one Lew Alcindor who would later morph into pro basketball legend Kareem Abdul Jabbar and Paul

Stanley who would grow up to front the rock band Kiss.

In the mid 70's, fresh out of University and with a child, this is what the Mirandas could afford and they were determined to make the best of it. They moved into a small apartment on Payson Street which bordered on Dyckman Street, a quiet but mildly lower and middle class neighborhood where the highlight of the day was people going to and from work. Inwood was ethnically diverse with an emphasis on Hispanic culture which was exactly what the Miranda family was looking for. In an interview with *NBC News*, Luis Miranda acknowledged that his wife and he had chosen Inwood because "It reflected a Puerto Rican style of culture that they wanted their children to be raised in."

They were able to navigate family and working life with relative ease, thanks, to a large extent, to the addition of a Puerto Rican relative, Edmundo Claudio, who immigrated to the states and became the Miranda's full time nanny. Which allowed Miranda's parents to actively pursue their passions as a child psychologist (Luz) and an up and coming political activist (Luis). In fact Miranda, looking back on his earliest memories of his childhood in *The New Yorker*, would chuckle as he recalled that, "My parents worked so much that I really remember them only on weekends."

When not working, The Mirandas, in their own subtle, matter of fact way, easily fit into the fabric of the community. One person who would occasionally come in contact with the Mirandas was their next door neighbor Jubel Raziel who recalled in an *Extra Newsfeed blog* that his meetings with the family were often fleeting.

"I grew up next door to the Miranda family," said Raziel. "I knew Lin's father. He was always a kind man who would say 'hi' to me whenever he saw me cleaning in front of my building. His mom was a quiet woman. The Miranda's family backyard and ours actually connected and I'd often jump into their yard to retrieve a ball my brother, myself or a friend would accidentally kick or hit into it. Lin's dad would occasionally stop and talk to my mom when she walked our dog."

Throughout the 70's and into the 80's, the Mirandas worked hard at their life. Luz was making great strides as a child psychologist while Luis, who had tossed aside his psychological leanings in favor of his early love of politics, saw the family's social capitol rise as his determination and drive eventually made him the go-to conduit between big city politicians and the increasing power and importance of the Hispanic community. People in the halls of New York politics were taking his calls and, most importantly, they were listening to what he had to say. Luis was racking up numerous credits as a consultant with high profile political personalities.

But at the end of the day, it was ultimately about family and, in 1980 the couple was overjoyed when they discovered that Luz was pregnant with their second child. There was a sense about this child that there would be something different, something that would play deeply in the sense of Puerto Rican pride and culture. And as the birth of their second child loomed closer, Luis and Luz turned to literature and the creative mind when it came to naming their child. One work of Puerto Rican literature struck a particular note with the couple.

Nana Roja Para Mi Hijo Lin-Manuel by the Puerto Rican author Jose Manuel Torres Santiago was a work that dug deep in the philosophy and depth of culture and family. And so on January 16, 1980 Lin-Manuel Miranda came kicking and screaming into the world.

Chapter Three
A Prodigy in the Works

Luis held a number of jobs growing up in Puerto Rico. Easily the most memorable and endearing was the time he spent selling records. He learned to appreciate the diverse sounds and musical styles and, in particular, the broad emotions and theatrical complexities that went into the soundtracks of Broadway plays and motion pictures. It was a love that would stay with him forever and follow him wherever he travelled.

Music followed Luis to America and, finally, it became the background and the rhythm of his life with his beloved Luz and daughter Luz in his home in Inwood. And music would be a vibe and emotion that would guide Miranda from the moment he opened his eyes and ears for the first time.

Miranda would often insist that, despite his Puerto Rican heritage, he was actually one quarter Mexican. While that maybe the case, his earliest experiences were definitely in line with his parents' Puerto Rican experiences and attitudes. Miranda found his earliest memories being of a chaotic household in which he basically saw his parents going to and coming from work. But Miranda's parents were doting parents and made the most of their time with their children.

Due to their growing notoriety in both political and academic circles, the Miranda household would often be an intellectual gathering point for the surrounding neighborhood. In looking back on those 'drawing room' get-togethers in a *Hispanic Scholarship.com* story, Miranda acknowledged that, "There were always politicians around the house, other teachers and community activists. Having that kind of education gave us, more than anything, an intellectual curiosity."

From the outset, Miranda and his sister were guided on a bilingual path, learning that to speak both English and Spanish was important to establishing cultural and academic footholds in America while hanging on tightly to their Puerto Rican heritage. Miranda gravitated toward the possibilities of his life and upbringing with relish. He and his sister, at a very young age, did not balk when their father taught them how to salsa dance. Luis acknowledged in a *New Yorker* interview that something as simple as learning to dance was an important part of his children's upbringing. "For me, it was very important that they learned how to dance."

Miranda's introduction to music, likewise, came in an informal and cultural way. The Miranda family was known in the neighborhood as the family that had grand parties in which traditional Puerto Rican music, as well as other forms of Latin pop and jazz often served as a background. As the parties inevitably wound down, Luis and Luz would regularly slip Broadway musical soundtracks onto their turntable as a kind of end of the night 'chaser.' Even at a very young age, the young Miranda was all ears.

By the time Miranda reached age three, he was

showcasing an innate sense of media and music and how it related to himself and his life. Movies, television, commercials and people speaking, all seemed to resonate to the young boy on a much deeper level of understanding and empathy than most three year olds could comprehend. And in Miranda's ever-expanding world there was a whole new sphere of music to be experienced. Miranda was a literal sponge as he soaked up the vibe and emotions of all forms of salsa, merengue, 80's style pop, rock and jazz. But it was his parents and their seemingly endless collection of show tunes that truly struck at the young boy's creative soul.

David Diggs, the actor who played Thomas Jefferson in the Broadway production of *Hamilton*, seemingly understated the obvious when he told *The New Yorker,* "He grew up engaged in musical theater."

While both of his parents were fully involved in guiding his early years in the creative arts, years later Miranda, in a conversation with *I Interview Playwrights.com*, would seemingly give the lion's share of the credit to his mother. "My mom did a good job with me. She saw me making up songs and writing stories and making flip books at a very young age and realized I was always filtering the world in some way. She would key into that tendency to get me to do things I didn't want to do. If it was a chore or a crappy job or even something tragic, she would say, 'Just think of the story you're going to get out of this. You could write a song about it.' And it gave me perspective at a very young age."

Around the house, the young Miranda seemed to have the soundtracks of *Jesus Christ: Superstar*, *Man of La Mancha* and such classic movie musicals as *The*

Sound of Music and *The Unsinkable Molly Brown* on a never-ending loop. It was a doable education and a substitute for a family that did not have a lot of money and rarely got out to see live theater. Miranda recalled his limited theatre experience when he related "The only shows I saw as a kid was that holy trinity of live theater, *Les Miz*, *Cats* and *Phantom of The Opera.*"

His love of music immediately became an influence that drove Miranda, still years away from formal education, to become a prodigy in the making. His father recalled in *The New Yorker* how it had quickly became evident that his young son was on the verge of being something special. "He was always very verbal. Lin was already reading by age three, three and a half. "We sent him to a local nursery school at age four. He was the only reader in the class so he would read to the other kids and the other kids would sort of gather around him because he was the one that would pick up a book."

Miranda's maturity beyond his years continued. His talents turned to the piano at age six. That he was quite good for a boy of six was not surprising to those in the Miranda family who had come to expect much more from this brighter than average child. What came as a surprise was that Miranda had deduced the cause and effect of his talent. Playing well was earning him positive feedback, applause and verbal pats on the back struck squarely at Miranda's ego. In a *New Yorker* conversation, Luis offered up a prime example of his son's first brush with stardom during an early creative coming out at Hunter Elementary School.

"His teacher put on a recital and each of the kids in Lin's class did a couple of songs. After Lin played his first song and people applauded, he played a second song and there was more applause. Suddenly he was like, 'I know another one' and we had to pull him away from the piano because he so loved the applause that he could not get enough of it."

Miranda's parents were perceptive people. It was incidents such as these that painted a picture of their son that indicated he was destined for greatness of some kind. Creatively and intellectually, they felt a regular public school would not challenge him and so Miranda's parents cast an eye toward Hunter College Elementary School, a school for the gifted within the New York City public school system.

A laudatory piece in *Business Insider* painted Hunter College Elementary School as the ultimate in exclusivity. Each year, the school selected, through a series of stringent entrance exams, 25 boys and 25 girls from a pool of 2500 kindergarten aged applicants to enter a system that was designed, specifically, to cultivate the creative potential of its students. It was harder to get into Hunter College Elementary than it was to get into Harvard. Miranda would make the cut. But it was with no small amount of trepidation and insecurity that the young boy entered his first day at school.

Miranda, even at that age, was perceptive enough to realize that he was different. A large percentage of his elementary school classmates were white and Jewish. At home, Miranda spoke primarily Spanish but, at Hunter, was required to speak what would be halting, less than confident English. Miranda was totally unsure of what Hunter would bring and how his life would play out--heavy thoughts for a boy so young.

But Miranda was very much a six-year-old realist when he assessed his elementary school days with *60 Minutes*.

"You know, I went to a school where everyone was smarter than me and I'm not just blowing smoke. I was surrounded by genius kids. What's interesting about growing up in a culture like that is you go, 'Alright, I've got to figure out what my thing is. Because I'm not smarter than these kids and I'm not funnier than half of them. So I better figure out what it is I wanna do and work really hard at that because, intellectually, I'm treading water to be here.'"

Miranda looked inward, to his gut, his heart and his soul. Instinctively, the six year old knew what drove him. He matter-of-factly recalled in his *60 Minutes* interview, his decision and started moving forward. "I just picked a lane and started running. And I finally decided, 'Well alright! This!'"

Chapter Four
Rapping on the Bus

Every time Miranda turned around, his world and, most importantly, his musical world appeared to be changing. Latin Music and show tunes continued to be his signposts up ahead, the place he wanted to be. But by the time he entered Hunter College Elementary School, Miranda's world and the music that drove him was taking a hard creative right turn.

Down a street populated by rap and hip hop.

"It was the music that was on the rise," Miranda told *The New York Times* of the encroachment of the music on his psyche. Miranda's sister, Luz, would be instrumental in his music education. Being older, she had already become quite familiar with the new music, consequently passing the sounds of The Fat Boys, The Beastie Boys and Eric B & Rakim to her younger brother. Luz also furthered Miranda's musical education by taking him to a screening of the pioneering rap film *Beat Street*. Miranda quickly latched onto the vibe of this rough hewn, yet lyrically out-there street sound.

"My sister is as responsible as anyone for giving me good taste in music," he acknowledged in a conversation with *National Public Radio*. "I remember stealing her copy of Black Sheep's *A Wolf in Sheep's Clothing* and learning the rap song 'Engine,' engine number 9, on the New York transit line.' It was the first rap song I learned all the way through."

Rap 101 would also be taught on a daily basis, courtesy of a bus driver.

Billy Baker Jr. drove a school bus between Inwood and Hunter College Elementary School on a daily basis. It was the way he made his living. But his real passion was rap and hip hop. He lived it and breathed it. And he was quick to impart his knowledge to the children who rode his bus, filling the time between pick up and drop off by teaching his impressionable young charges the lyrics to his favorite rap and hip hop songs. In Miranda, he had a particularly rapt and receptive audience. Miranda proved a quick study in this impromptu course and was soon reciting the often rough and raw lyrics of Boogie Down Productions, Ceto Boys and The Sugarhill Gang.

But all the outside influences in his world could not have prepared Miranda for the magic of Hunter College Elementary School. For Miranda, Hunter presented the perfect entry into a world he already desired but, at age six, could not completely fathom. Already an arts oriented institution, the year Miranda entered was highlighted by the addition of a brand new music teacher named Barbara Ames whose enthusiasm for teaching was matched by her progressive nature.

"The impact of arts education really saved my life," said an effusive Miranda in a *WFMT.com* interview. "There my life was really changed by a school music teacher named Barbara Ames. The accident of timing could not have been more perfect "

Ames, with the help of the school's shop teacher,

Robert Sherman, instituted what would come to be called the 'Sixth Grade Play' in which each year's sixth grade class would end the year with the entire school gathering to watch the sixth grade class put on a play. That each succeeding year would offer up a brand new theatrical experience for the lower grades would turn out to be the perfect learning experience for the young Miranda.

"I saw *Westside Story* when I was in kindergarten," he recalled to *WFMT.com.*" In the first grade, I saw *Fiddler on The Roof.* In the second grade, I saw a mash up of *Wizard of Oz* and *The Whiz.* By second grade I was already thinking 'What's our play going to be when we're sixth graders?' So my brain was already wired to school culminating in a musical. In the third grade, it was *Peter Pan*, fourth grade *Oklahoma*, fifth grade, *Bye Bye Birdie.* Our entire class was vibrating at this point with the question 'What is our sixth grade play going to be?'"

Miranda's excitement would translate into amazingly proficient and little known projects away from school. A literal treasure trove of long lost videos has surfaced over the years, often conceived and shot in front of a bedroom mirror that showcased the youngster creating freestyle moments, Latin style covers of pop songs, a video of his playing Jesus Christ in a snippet of the musical *Jesus Christ Superstar* and singing and dancing in mini videos of the title song from *Footloose* and the group Go West's King of Wishful Thinking. Easily his most ambitious childhood project was the video book report of the novel *The Pushcart War.* An ambitious project by eight year-old standards, Miranda, exercised potent acting chops playing the title character Max Hammerman while directing his mother, sister and great grandmother in big and small moments. For his efforts, Miranda received an A.

As it would turn out, Miranda was not the only one excited about the possibilities at Hunter Elementary. Teachers Ames and Sherman had some questions of their own as Miranda's sixth grade play loomed in the coming year. They had discovered that they had suddenly run out of age appropriate musicals for elementary school children. To solve the problem, the teachers went to a summer instructional class for teachers where they worked on the idea of writing musical with the kids. When school started and the new approach was presented to the class, their response, as explained by Miranda to *WFMT.com* was less than enthusiastic.

"We replied 'No!' We've been working our entire lives to do a musical that someone else wrote."

Halfway through the school year and Ames and Sherman could see that writing their own play might not have been the best idea. The children were complaining and not much was getting done so they ultimately decided on a compromise that would go under the title of *Four Plus Six By Six Grade* that would comprise the six years of the school's previous musicals plus four original student written compositions.

Four Plus Six By Six Grade would be a smashing, if extremely long (at four plus hours) sixth grade success. Miranda was all over the cast credits, to wit Conrad Birdie in *Bye Bye Birdie*, a cow hand in *Oklahoma*, a son in *Fiddler on The Roof*, Captain

Hook in *Peter Pan*, Bernardo in *Westside Story* and an Addaperle backup In *The Wizard of Oz* and *The Whiz*.

It was in the role of Conrad Birdie, the gyrating rock star in *Bye Bye Birdie* that Miranda would most fondly recall to *WMFT*, "At Hunter I received a very lethal dosage of musical theater at a very young age. I got to play literally all the parts and I realized that it was the best time of my life. At the time *Bye Bye Birdie* might not have looked like much But gyrating around in that gold lame suit and having every girl in the sixth grade pretend to faint and fall in love with you, this was the moment that I realized that I would be doing this for the rest of my life."

Chapter Five
Between Two Worlds

That Miranda would grow up literally a part of two distinctive and seemingly polar opposite worlds was by design. His parents did not want their son to become another casualty of assimilation, trying so hard to fit an American mold that he would discard his Puerto Rican roots. Consequently, growing up in the neighborhood, Miranda would speak, primarily Spanish around the house while managing a fair bit of English everywhere else. But ultimately, the Latino influence would be where his heart and soul would land when growing up as a child in Inwood.

"I've always relaxed more in my neighborhood because I know where all the stuff is," he told *Vibe*. "I feel comfortable with the noise and seeing other Latinos around me. There's an ease I feel from 168th Street to the end of the island that I don't feel anywhere else on Earth."

Miranda's father, always a bit philosophical about such matters, chalked up their parenting style to a sense of history in a conversation with *NBC News*. "It was the closest we came to giving the kids the feeling of a close knit Puerto Rican town. History determines which way the future will go. Without that history, one lives as if one were in quicksand, in a world that has no context."

Miranda, with no small amount of guidance from his parents, had an instinctive feel for his world and proved a quick learner when it came to potential pitfalls. Consequently, the young boy knew his neighborhood well. He discovered that there were areas that were unsafe to venture into, places that bred trouble and dead end lives, and he avoided them. Even if he sensed he was in a place that could cause him trouble, he was quick to turn tail and run the other way. At the other end of his mental lesson plan, there were the good times with good people, playing dominos with people on a stoop or just plain hanging out. In Miranda's world, there was nary a hint of trouble.

But as his neighbor Jubei Raziel would relate in an *Extra Newsfeed blog,* Miranda would often present a rather striking figure to his neighbors. "Lin was that strange kid who wore dark clothes, a beanie hat and was always wearing headphones, walking to the beat of whatever he was listening to. He usually appeared disinterested with the world around him."

Raziel's assessment was spot on for Miranda was seemingly enveloped in a world of fantasy at a very young age and, in a metaphoric sense, was running into its arms at every opportunity as he would recall in an interview with *National Public Radio*. "I had the great joy of being nine years old when *The Little Mermaid* came out. I went and saw it three times in the theater and then I dragged my parents and my family back to see it a couple of more times."

And when he wasn't enthralled and enraptured by the images of Disney, he always had the songs of soundtracks, films and pop music to while away the hours. Miranda's mother related to Charlie Rose that her son "loved to sing. He was always creating and he loved words and songs." And Miranda would readily acknowledge that songs would mentally occupy his world 24/7. "Music was in my head all the time," he told Charlie Rose. "Because I had a lot of time on my hands."

Miranda saw the dichotomy of his life as a Puerto Rican in America at a very early age and he acknowledged his reality in an interview with *Grantland.com*, that much of how he played out his life in two different worlds of influence, the ethnic vs. the American, was set in motion the day he showed up at the doorstep of Hunter College Elementary at age six.

"I got to Hunter College Elementary when I was six years old. So, already it was like they call me Lin at school and Lin-Manuel at home. It was also super stark when there was another language involved. I spoke Spanish at home and English at school. The people I knew from the neighborhood were primarily Latin but I've had all white Jewish friends from the time I was six years old."

However, Miranda's parents were not about to let their son forget his roots. During the summer months, Miranda would make an annual pilgrimage to his father's home town in Puerto Rico and would spend time living among and learning from his father's still thriving, extended family. And so armed with only passable Spanish language skills and a whole lot of enthusiasm and curiosity, Miranda would spend one month each year absorbing yet another aspect of his culture.

Years later in a *Spokesman.com* feature, Miranda

would look back on those trips in philosophical tones. "When you're born in the United States, but your parents are from Puerto Rico, you always live a double life. And that's a good way to be because you're always observing the differences between Puerto Rico and New York."

What the young Miranda found during those stays were clues to his parents' lives and attitudes. Much like his father, the Miranda family was industrious and hard working, often holding down a myriad of jobs and finding little time for idle moments. On one such trip, the young boy got into the spirit of the family's work ethic when, for a time, he took up selling ice cream on a street corner. But given the fact that his relatives were always working and his limited Spanish skills made it difficult to make friends outside the family circle, Miranda often found himself alone and left to his own devices. Which was fine with the boy because his mind was working overtime at this point, creating a literal dervish of plays, musical happenings and an untold number of flights of fancy to amuse himself and, often by association, family members and neighbors who happened to be around when Miranda, creatively, was "on."

One of the more somewhat willing and bemused foils for Miranda's Puerto Rican antics was the neighbor woman Margot Rodriguez who related in an *Associated Press* article some of Miranda's more madcap moments that she was involved in. In one instance, she related that Miranda thrust a broom handle in her hands and made her pretend to play guitar while he sang. She also recounted the time he used her as an actress, urging her to scream as he threw a makeshift puppet from a tree, pretending it was he who had fallen.

"He would come up with the craziest things," she told *The Associated Press*. "I love that boy."

Chapter Six
Rising Up from the Back Row

Following the creative surge that Miranda experienced throughout his elementary school years, the feeling was that Miranda would soar to even greater heights entering Hunter College's middle school and high school programs. But noticeably absent from his seventh grade classes was anything to do with theater. Not that Miranda had suddenly burned out. He would continue to write, often for his own amusement, and was becoming fairly proficient as a musician. But when it came to getting on stage and creating live performance, Miranda was nowhere to be found.

Miranda has never, satisfactorily, explained the year away from theater but just going on the assumption that Miranda was a fairly normal 12 year old going on 13, the distraction factor would most likely have been high. He did hint at the isolation he may well have been feeling in an *Educational Theatre Association* piece when he recalled sitting in the back of his English class "writing a bunch of stuff, none of which was for the class. I was writing a lot of bad love songs that were for girls." In a *Kennedy Center.org* conversation, he also hinted that while he was often distracted during his year in eighth grade, he was, in fact, quietly doing his own thing in a stealth manner. "I spent most of eighth grade scribbling song lyrics and poems in the back of my class and earning grades just good enough to get by. I never saw any reason to share these with anyone else."

Hunter College High School being the socially and artistically inclined community most gifted schools were, Miranda's absence from the theater program and his seemingly 'going through the motions' in his other classes became noticeable among the students and faculty. Of the latter, an English teacher named Rembert Herbert, who had Miranda in eighth grade English, took particular notice.

Herbert was a creatively savvy instructor, alternately intuitive and deeply insightful when it came to students. Consequently, he offered in a note he scribbled on the back of a Miranda class assignment "I have suspected for some time that you have been 'hibernating' in the back of my class."

But Miranda was more than capable, even in his most 'down' moments of creative brilliance, as witness the essay and class assignment that brought Herbert's notes. For a semester project in eighth grade English, Miranda and the rest of the class' project for the semester was for each student was to teach three chapters of the book *The Chosen* by Chaim Potok as part of a group. Miranda had loved the way Herbert had taught the book, looking beyond a literal telling and challenging his students to find the connections and the themes for themselves. Not surprisingly, Miranda did not take the easy or conventional approach to the assignment.

"I decided it would be a lot easier to write a song

based on each chapter and have our group perform it," Miranda reflected in an homage to his eighth grade English teacher in the *Kennedy Center.org.* "Actually, I recorded myself singing all the songs and made my group mates lip-synch my voice as I had no trust in their musical ability and no way of teaching it to them."

Herbert thought Miranda's interpretation was "excellent and well crafted" in his note congratulating the young boy. Miranda related in *Kennedy Center.org* that his teacher had essentially called him out. "He told me that the creative energy you are burning in the back of the class is what we need in the class. You can use that here."

Miranda still gets a bit misty eyed when he remembered how Herbert concluded the note. "He was the first person outside of my family to say to me 'You are a good writer.'"

Herbert was not the only instructor who would become an influence in Miranda's high school years. Especially as it pertained to any thoughts of Hamilton. Irv Steinfink, a veteran teacher at Hunter High School, was quite familiar with Miranda, having the young student in his homeroom class and as a student in his 11th grade Social Studies class. In a 2017 interview with this author, Steinfink painted a picture of Miranda as a model student.

"He was quiet in my class," the teacher acknowledged. "He didn't speak up a lot. He was cooperative and he never acted out. He was always engaged in his work and he always gave concise answers when I asked him questions. What I knew about him outside of my class was that he was in theatre and that he was quite talented."

Hamilton would come into Miranda's worldview during a big part of his social studies' semester grade as recalled Steinfink. "The assignment I gave the class was a major research assignment in which the class had all semester to write on any topic they wanted. I went around the room and asked each student what they might be interested in. When I got to Lin, he had no idea. He couldn't come up with anything at all. So I said 'think about it and I'll come back to you'. So I went around the room and I came back to Lin and he still had no idea."

Steinfink had a suggestion. Years previously, he had done quite a bit of research and had written a big paper on the legendary Hamilton-Burr duel. "So I recommended that he do his paper on the Hamilton duel. His response was, 'Oh yeah. That sounds good.'"

Steinfink monitored Miranda's progress on the paper at various points during the semester. "I know we talked about it at various points during the semester and he seemed very interested in what he was doing. Obviously this was some years before the Chernow book on Hamilton came out but he was diligent in using research from a number of other historians on the subject."

The final paper was everything that Steinfink could have hoped for and a whole lot more. "He did a very good job. It was a good paper. He got an A on it. As I think about it now, it may have actually been an A plus."

Chapter Seven
Brick Prison

Herbert's and Steinfink's pronouncements were all the encouragement Miranda seemingly needed to come to a life decision about his future in music and theater. He was only in the eighth grade but, as he offered in a *WFMT* interview, he was now all in. "I thought 'I am doing this for the rest of my life if they will let me.'"

Herbert was quite willing to give him a well-meaning nudge in that direction when he pointed his young charge in the direction of the student run theatrical club called Brick Prison. In a school long known as one of the hippest, Brick Prison, whose productions were known for their cutting edge independent streak and where the coolest of the cool kids wrote, directed and acted with nary a hint of adult supervision. Brick Prison was largely the domain of juniors and seniors but Herbert insisted that he had the creative chops to act in Brick Prison productions.

It did not take long for Miranda to make a home in Brick Prison as a budding actor. He already knew some of the club members informally and had formed a fairly tight friendship with a ninth grader named Chris Harris who grew up to host a top rated news program on *MSNBC*. Soon Miranda had risen up the

Brick Prison hierarchy to a point where on a Saturday afternoon, he found himself rehearsing for a role in his very first high school play.

It was during a break in that rehearsal that Herbert, who was monitoring the club, told the seniors in charge that he felt Miranda should be writing musicals for Brick Prison. Miranda felt mortified, lowering his head as the rest of the club eyed him wearily. All the by then 16 year old could manage was "What?" The creative gauntlet had effectively been thrown down. And Miranda would pick it up and run with it.

Classmate Hayes was one of the earliest converts to Miranda's world view who directed a very early Miranda penned 20 minute musical called *Nightmare in D Major*, a very Freudian and ambitious musical journey that totally impressed and surprised Hayes. But, as he explained in *Chrishayes.org,* not totally. "I realized that my friend was a genius when he was 13. When I was a senior in high school I had the pleasure of directing the very first musical written by Lin who had, by that time, grown into a ludicrously talented friend. *Nightmare in D Major* was about the extended dream of a protagonist named Dylan and the music was shockingly good."

Miranda would follow that up with a short piece about a seventh grader's first kiss at an unchaperoned party called *Seven Minutes in Heaven*. For Miranda, creativity continued to be spontaneous and, in the case of *Seven Minutes in Heaven*, it struck in some seemingly unorthodox places. "I wrote *Seven Minutes in Heaven*, my senior year musical, on a piano that sat next to the nurses' office," he recalled in a Twitter entry.

When not writing, Miranda became a first rate actor who, throughout his high school years, was a regular in both productions by Hunter's theater arts department and Brick Prison. Miranda's enthusiasm for what was turning into his 'wonder years' was much in evidence as he ticked off his greatest high school hits in conversation with the *Educational Theatre Association*.

"I was in Lillian Hellman's *The Little Foxes* and in the play *You Can't Take It With You*. In the ninth grade I got cast as The Pirate King in *The Pirates of Penzance*. That was a huge deal for me because I beat out the seniors for the part. Then *Godspell* in tenth grade. I started dating the assistant director of *Godspell* and she became my high school girlfriend. Then she directed *A Chorus Line* in my junior year and I was her assistant director so I kind of apprenticed into the directing track. Then I kind of had my big break when I directed *West Side Story* in my senior year."

Miranda looked upon his sojourn into *West Side Story* as an important personal journey. Despite its long and respected history, *West Side Story* was still considered controversial in many critical quarters because of its depiction of Puerto Rican and American gang members as losers with little if any hope. But Miranda, barely 18 at the time, saw beyond the obvious and, in his direction, wanted to bring some depth and, if he were lucky, a broader understanding of Puerto Ricans and their culture into a predominantly white American worldview.

An important step in Miranda's production was that he brought his father in to the school to give dialect lessons to both the white and Asian students who would be playing the Sharks. Miranda turned up his nose at the notion of anything connected to his directing debut being anything but professional in its concept and execution. He related in *Education Theatre Association* that "I wanted to make sure that while they're in America, they [the gang members] are yelling Puerto Rican things like 'Wepa!' It was a way for me to actually engage the part of me that only existed at home and bring it into school."

Encouraged by the creative rewards of theatre, Miranda eventually began to experiment with making short films in and around the Hunter High School campus where his notoriety and popularity in the theatre department and Brick Prison gave him a regular list of people willing to cast and crew his productions.

And while he was keeping his fairly tight to his theatre interests, Miranda was also dabbling in the musical side of things. He took a class in orchestration and composition because it was offered but limited his practical application to piano lessons and basic musical theory. But, like every element of his creative side, Miranda was serious enough to practice all hours of the day and night. Which inevitably led to midnight calls to musically inclined friends with questions about the viability of certain chords. He would frequently become excited at the possibility of having discovered a new chord. But as he acknowledged in *American Theatre Association*, that bubble was usually burst. "I didn't know what a chord was called and I kept thinking I was going to invent a new chord. And they would say 'No, they all exist.'"

Chapter Eight
Cool Cats and Garbage Cans

Miranda became aware of what societal rules in high school were all about. And to a large extent, Hunter College High School was typical of what all high schools had been since the dawn of time. There was the hierarchy, the mid level serfs vying for attention and finally the bottom feeders, those anxious for any bit of recognition, and looking for any way of getting through the day, let alone the semester, without too many emotional scars. Kind of like *Lord of The Flies* with a hall pass and a lunch break instead of a pig's head on a stack.

Miranda had gotten lucky. He was a Theatre Kid. And Theatre Kids basically operated by their own set of rules. Miranda broke it down during a conversation with *Educational Theatre Association*. "The saving grace of being a Theatre Kid is that you get to make friends in every grade. If your grade was kicking your butt, which was true for me some of the time, I had friends in other grades. The heartbreak that comes with that is sometimes your best friend will graduate because they are two or three years older than you."

In the same interview, Miranda acknowledged that he was quick to pick up on how things worked in

Hunter's hallways and classrooms. "They [fellow students] were relentlessly involved with who is friends with who, what clique is big and who's in and who's out in my grade. Being a Theatre Kid allows you to have this bird's eye view of it. I would spend my lunch period with at least four different groups. So I was always a friend with everyone."

Miranda had managed a rep on campus. He was the kid who carried a boom box with him everywhere he went. He was the kid who wrote the school musicals and plays. But, perhaps most importantly to Miranda's drive to succeed, was that he was the Latino kid in a school that was not Latino. Miranda looked back on his high school image as 'a cool cat' in a *New York Times* wedding announcement as a stance born of circumstance. "You either try to blend in or you overcompensate."

Which ultimately translated into being a cool and sometimes unusual boy about campus as a coping mechanism as he explained in a *New York Times* homage to the late *Rent* creator Jonathan Larson. "Everyone has their own coping mechanisms for surviving high school. Mine was showing up every day with a VHS camcorder and making movies, because I found it so much easier than talking to other kids. It's much easier to say 'I'm making a movie and I have a part for you' than 'Wanna hang out?'"

But when it came to high school romance and affairs of the heart, Miranda admitted that he was often not up to the task. "I've always been famously bad at talking to women I find attractive," he told the *New York Times*. "I had a total lack of game."

Which meant that, like most other teenage boys, he spent the time looking at girls across the schoolyard and thinking sometimes chaste, sometimes lustful thoughts. In Miranda's case, one object of his affections was one Vanessa Nadal who was attractive, intelligent and definitely above his emotional pay grade. By all accounts, Miranda's first serious girlfriend who remains unidentified to this day, came into his life as a junior in Hunter. It appeared to be a classic mix. Both were heavily into theatre and creating. They had the same tastes in music, media and pop culture. And what is finally known is that it would be a relationship that would last, in varying degrees, for a number of years.

It was inevitable that as Miranda grew through his school years, his relationship with the people in his community would change. Although a 'homeboy' with a love for the community and people he grew up with, and somebody who continued to walk the streets of Inwood in comfort and ease, it became noticeable, eventually to Miranda himself, that his worldview was stretching far beyond his neighborhood streets and bodegas. "The neighborhood kids would chill on the corner and I would see them when I took out the recycling on Fridays."

On the surface, Miranda always seemed perpetually upbeat with that impish grin and good-natured attitude constants in his physical and psychological makeup. In hindsight, Miranda would have you believe that it was a good cover-up because, as he would admit in a *GQ* interview that delved deep into his psyche as a creative, that while he has gotten better with dealing with his dark side, his early years were marked by a preoccupation with death.

"I was very preoccupied, my entire childhood and

into my teens, with death. I would get into a relationship and I would imagine the ways my date could have died on the way home which, to my mind, was like 'Well that's realistic. Nothing is fucking promised.'"

But there was more to Miranda's wonder years than angst and dark thoughts. By the time the youngster had reached his teens, he had quite the psychological arsenal to get through his high school years relatively unscathed. And the biggest element in his trick bag was that Miranda could be funny at the drop of a hat. Hanging around Miranda was to be bombarded by glib commentary, ironic asides and all manner of one liners and comic observations. As he explained in a *New Yorker* conversation, Miranda was smart that way.

"The currency that matters around smart kids is funny. If you can be funny, you're going to be fine. So I got really funny."

However being funny was not the perfect shield. Miranda had his Kryptonite in human form and it came in the guise of a skulking, mean spirited bully named Felipe Andres Coronel who in later years would gain another kind of reputation as the notorious rapper Immortal Technique whose modus operandi of terror was to throw his victims in a garbage can. Miranda gave up his bullying memories in a laugh filled conversation with the podcast *WTF*. "He was our school bully," he chuckled. "He terrorized kids. He threw them in garbage cans. I got thrown in a garbage can. He was a really angry kid."

Miranda's good buddy Hayes told *Viceland* that what Miranda had recently brought to light was all true. "Felipe was kind of a bully back in the day. He would do things like put people in trashcans and sing the song *Bucktown*. He didn't have any discernible politics other than beating up my friends."

With the bully charges suddenly reemerging, Immortal Technique felt obligated to give his side of the story in an interview with *Complex*. "All of that was a story about personal growth and redemption and people twisted it into Lin and I being long time adversaries. We have always been very proud of each other's success and have even joked about all the bullying stuff with each other. I appreciative to say that today we are friends."

But Miranda still busts up at the memory of the time Felipe ventured onto Lin's turf. "He got a part in our senior year in a class play and I was like, 'Oh my God! I'm in a fucking play with that dude who scares the shit out of me and all my friends.'"

Miranda's drive and, yes, no small amount of ego, always seemed to put him on the edge of something new, different and challenging and his often outrageous pronouncements and ideas had come to become a part of a daily life experience for those in Miranda's inner circle. And so nobody was overly surprised when, shortly after Miranda turned 15, he announced that he was going to make a movie.

After they stopped laughing and rolling their eyes, many were quickly recruited into Miranda's brainstorm of a project, an extremely no budget comedy mystery entitled *Clayton's Friends*, the story of an overnight teen party that takes an unexpected turn when people begin to disappear. Miranda produced, directed and wrote what would turn out to be a miniscule 59 minute movie. And the results as explained by a candid Miranda in *This Is New York.com* were less than Oscar-worthy.

"I made a movie when I was 15 years old with all my friends. This was back when IMDB was a little more lax in its proceedings and so *Clayton's Friends* is listed as my very first project. It's a terrible movie. I wrote 50 percent of the script because I had always wanted to kiss this one girl and I wrote a kissing scene with that girl into the script."

Chapter Nine
Life Changing

Miranda was a babe in the woods when it came to live theatre. He had certainly memorized a literal library of cast albums. But when it came to the live experience of a Broadway production, money had always been tight and so, in his 17 years, he had only experienced Broadway productions of *Les Miserables*, *Phantom of The Opera* and *Cats*. However on the occasion of his 17th birthday, all that was about to change.

His high school sweetheart, Meredith, had surprised him with the best seats very little money could buy. Last row of the second mezzanine of the Nederlander Theater for a performance of the musical *Rent*. The curtain went up and Miranda was immediately overwhelmed by sights and sounds he had never experienced before.

"Suddenly here I was seeing a musical that took place not in a far off land or in a far off country," he said in *NEA Magazine*, "but in the West Village with people struggling with the question of whether to stay in the arts or sell out. People were struggling with disease and poverty. It was the New York struggle in musical form and it took place now."

Miranda was immediately bowled over by the fact

that the diverse ethnic cast was just like him and the people he met in life. The language and the music were street to him in a very real sense. Miranda's preconceived notion of what musical theater could be was turned on its head. "I think that seeing *Rent* tacitly gave me permission to write about what I know," he told *NEA Mag*. "*Rent* told me that I could write musicals."

Miranda returned to Hunter a creatively changed person and plunged immediately into a writing frenzy that saw him churn out a series of one-act musicals that played largely off the rocking influential blueprint laid down by *Rent*. There was a sense of deep-seated realism and electricity in those later high school efforts. The feedback from students and faculty was good. Miranda could not have been more confident at that moment that his future was being laid out before him.

Miranda graduated from Hunter High School in 1998 and chose well-known Wesleyan liberal and arts centered university in Middletown, Connecticut to further his education. Miranda had initially planned on a double major at Wesleyan, film and theater. But at this point, the lure of the stage and the possibilities of creating live theater proved too great and the incoming freshman dropped film studies with the stated goal of writing musicals.

On the personal front, Miranda's relationship with Meredith had survived through graduation but when Meredith ended up going to a different college, things appeared a bit shaky. They were continuing on as boyfriend/girlfriend but not seeing each other as often. Of more immediate importance to Miranda and, by association his parents, was that as their son entered Wesleyan, just as their daughter Luz was completing her studies, Luis and Luz had suddenly found themselves with financial concerns.

Getting their children the best possible education was an uppermost concern. But the best possible education was coming at a price. Luis, who had founded a not for profit, highly influential not for profit Latino organization, was forced to quit his own job to go into the more lucrative private sector. For her part, Luz had increased her already considerable workload and was now seeing patients seven days a week.

Miranda was keenly aware of his family's financial difficulties as he recalled to *The New York Times.* "Once, when my older sister announced that she might need an extra semester to graduate, my mother burst into tears at the kitchen table." His guilt at what his parents sacrificed had never been far from Miranda's thoughts, as witness a recollection in a commencement speech he delivered at Wesleyan in 2015. "My education was their second mortgage," he reflected. "And they were killing themselves to afford it."

The importance of achieving his goals was uppermost in his mind as he entered the Wesleyan University campus on that first day. "Wesleyan is a great school if you kind of know what you want to do with your life," he reflected in an *I Interview Playwrights.com* conversation. "I knew I loved theater and I knew I loved film and Wesleyan had great resources in both departments, enough so that I could say 'Spending my time here was going to be really important for me.' I was so hyper aware of the steep price my parents were paying that I knew I wanted to leave college with more than a diploma under my arm."

Miranda was encouraged by the wide-open

possibilities of the theater department as personified by the in-house production company Second Stage. He discovered that he could write something, apply to Second Stage for a budget and get it produced in a matter of months. Miranda was not going to waste any time. He jumped feet first into the Wesleyan theater scene.

Miranda was very active in his freshman year, appearing as an actor in two school musicals and a play and directing his own 20-minute musical. And, along the way, he was discovering that the chasm between high school and college was a big one. "I got to college thinking I knew everything," he reflected in *Educational Theatre Association*. "I got the rude awakening of 'Oh, I don't know anything. I know how theater at my high school worked. But there's still so much that I have to learn.'"

And by the time the now 20 year-old Miranda reached his sophomore year at Wesleyan, his personal life was also evolving. Meredith's educational path was entailing more and more time abroad. The couple of better than four years was seeing each other less and less. And whether he wanted to admit it or not, Miranda was beginning to grow and evolve beyond that relationship.

A big step for Miranda came when he moved into the University's Latino community living house, La Casa de Albizu Campos, ground zero for a small but thriving Latino community whose members were dedicated, on many levels, to a redefinition of Latino culture and experience. For Miranda, who had seemingly spent his entire life bouncing back and forth between Latin and American identities, living in what he lovingly referred to as La Casa would be an eye-opening experience. For the first time, Miranda was dealing with Latino friends who were also first generation Americans who were largely involved in their culture and experience. In this setting, Miranda constantly found himself in intellectual discussions and debates that, quite literally, opened up a whole new way of thinking and feeling about himself and where he came from.

More and more, cultural identity became of growing importance to him. In a documentary *In the Heights: Chasing Broadway Dreams*, Miranda was succinct in describing what it was that he had discovered. "The question of finding home is not only a geographical one but an emotional one. What does it mean to be Puerto Rican if you don't live in Puerto Rico?"

It was not long before Miranda was inspired to take his newfound ideals and beliefs to the stage and so, for much of his sophomore year, he used every spare moment to jot down notes and play with musical ideas that would become the musical *In the Heights*.

In the Heights chronicled three brutally hot days in the Latin community of Washington Heights in which stories of love, disappointment, frustration and all manner of emotions weave in and out of a driving, modern music beat. Bodega owner Usnavi is in a complex relationship with salon worker Vanessa. Nina has returned to the neighborhood with the news that she is dropping out of college and promptly falls in love with Benny who works for Nina's parents who are on the verge of selling their car service business to pay for her college education. All of the drama is in a constant circle around the play's central thematic core.

Should the central characters leave their neighborhood forever or, on a myriad of emotional levels, should they stay and fight?

"When I started writing it, no one was taking my words seriously," Miranda told *Swarthmore.com*. "I was just 20 years old and I was just writing a story that I wanted to write. I really wanted it to feel honest to my experience. My experience was not about Latinos and crime. I felt that Latinos and crime were very overrepresented. I didn't feel the need to represent that at all."

The process was gradual, Miranda's ever-present a notebook and the constant encouragement of friends helped the words and music fill the pages. Miranda was driven and, perhaps, a bit obsessed. His feelings about his work had taken a positive turn. He kept writing.

There was a lot of angst and questioning of his cultural life and times as the pages and the notebook began to reflect a story that was very much a tale of hope and home. "A lot of the show comes out of the theme of home and what we define as home," Miranda told *Playbill.com*. What do we take with us? What traditions do we pass on to our kids?"

It was sometime during his sophomore year at Wesleyan that Miranda had crafted an 80-minute, two act version of *In the Heights*. He offered *Playbill.com* his earliest assessment of his very first draft of *In the Heights*. "At that point, I had what I felt was a really good college show."

During the writing of *In the Heights*, he discovered that he had also developed a mysterious and extremely painful pain in his right shoulder.

People who knew chalked it up to writer's cramp and stress, the usual suspects. All Miranda knew was that the pain was getting worse.

Meredith returned home from yet another semester abroad. Miranda was ecstatic at the prospect of having quality time with his true love. It was a good time for the couple, marred only by the worsening pain in his shoulder. Miranda's parents were well aware of the worsening condition and, eventually, his mother insisted that he go to a highly recommended back specialist. In a riveting Wesleyan commencement speech he would give some years later, Miranda, for the first time, would reveal the particulars of that episode for the first time.

"The doctor examines me, looks me dead in the eyes and says 'There's nothing wrong with your back. What you have is a nervous tic. Is there anything in your life that is causing you stress?' I burst into tears. He looks me in the eyes and tells me 'You're trying to avoid going through pain or causing pain. I'm here to tell you that you'll have to survive it if you want to be any kind of artist.' "

Miranda weighed the doctor's words as he left the office. The pain was still there but he now felt a deep, psychological reason for it. What he would do next would ultimately challenge a lot of the preconceived notions and subconscious thoughts he had been harboring for years. He broke up with Meredith that same night.

But Miranda's psychological ordeal was far from over. He had a sense of the root cause of the pain but, again at his parent's insistence, would spend a number of months in intense therapy where his soul would, literally be laid bare. Miranda acknowledged in his commencement speech that "he told a lot of stories' during his months of therapy but he discovered that there was one basic truth that would finally result in the pain going away.

"The story I had been telling myself, a happy guy in a long distance relationship with his high school sweetheart, was being physically rejected by my body via my shoulder. I'd never broken up with anyone before. In my head, I was a good guy and good guys don't break up with their significant others when one of them goes off to study abroad. I was trying to fit my life into a romantic narrative that was increasingly at odds with how I really felt.

"In retrospect, Meredith and I both were."

Chapter Ten
In City Dreams

Miranda's shoulder stopped hurting about the time he emerged from therapy a new man. There were moments of longing for his lost love but he was confident that he'd made the right personal decision. Frustration and doubt were now in his rearview mirror. His creative future was up ahead, burning bright on the horizon.

Miranda would continue to be involved in all things theater throughout the remainder of his sophomore year but the very rough, raw and creatively uncooked first incarnation of *In the Heights* was never far from his thoughts. He was confident that this first serious step was the beginning of a new phase in his life and would be daring in bringing *In the Heights* out into the light.

"In the winter of 1999, I applied to Second Stage to put up a new show in the student run '92 Theater," he related in *Broadway.com*. "At the time I had one song and the title *In the Heights*. Second Stage accepted my proposal and I was given the theater for the weekend of April 20-22. Now all I had to do was write a show."

One of the first to see Miranda at work on *In the*

Heights was good friend Owen Panettieri who met Miranda during his sophomore year at Wesleyan when the two bonded over the production *Jesus Christ Superstar* in which Miranda played Jesus and Panettieri played Pilot. Panettieri, who described Miranda as "very easygoing and very friendly" in the very deep and detailed podcast *Broadway Backstory*, recalled how he came to be involved in the very first informal reading of *In the Heights* in the fall of 1999.

"He did maybe a song and a scene that he was developing from *In the Heights*. I read one of the parts and there were two songs. I read one of the parts and I sang one of the songs in a scene that included the characters Benny and Lincoln and the night they were having. So that was the very first thing that was done at Wesleyan with that."

Miranda totally immersed himself in the process of getting *In the Heights* ready for its debut during Wesleyan's winter break. He was not out and about like he usually was. While not totally reclusive in any sense, Miranda quite literally threw himself into *In the Heights* as he explained in *Broadway.com*. "I barely slept. I barely ate. I just wrote. I put in all the things I'd always wanted to see onstage. Propulsive freestyle rap scenes outside of bodegas, salsa numbers that also revealed. I tried to write the kind of show I'd want to be in."

As he would later reflect in *Latina.com*, his thoughts while writing that first true incarnation of *In the Heights* were never far from the music and how it would impact story and character. "I started with the music I heard around me my whole life. I saw the music as being the driving force behind the play."

The days and weeks leading up to *In the Heights'* official unveiling were reportedly a blur of excitement, fear and a first time introduction to Miranda as to what it took to mount a major production. Casting, synching the music, production duties and, most importantly, rehearsals seemed to spiral around the clock When it was determined that all the school's musicians would not be available to perform live during the show's short run, Miranda had the musicians record all the music beforehand for the cast to sing along to. In Miranda's mind, it was all creative madness but he felt that he was up to the task.

April 27. The curtain was about to go up on the very first public performance of *In the Heights*. Miranda was convinced that it was ready and that he had prepared for his maiden voyage. As he waited backstage and looked out into a theater filled to capacity, mentally he must have crossed himself.

The production of *In the Heights* presented at the '92 Theater consisted of one act, a total of 14 songs and, according to reviews seemed to focus largely on the central love story. The audience immediately and enthusiastically embraced it. A broad grin most certainly crossed Miranda's face as he reminisced about opening night with *Latina.com* "I remember in the early performances at Wesleyan how everyone would just lean into the stage and really perk up when the hip hop parts came about. For them it was something new."

Miranda's friend Panettieri recalled the rock concert-like excitement on opening night with *Broadway Backstory*. "The production was a huge hit. It was very, very popular. The line for the show was enormous. It was really crazy, even by the typical standard of what a student theater production would be. Everybody, at that point, really knew Lin in the theater community."

In the Heights' three-performance run was a resounding success, breaking attendance records for all Second Stage productions that year. Among those in attendance were two Wesleyan seniors, John Buffalo Mailer and Neil Stewart who were knocked out by the performance but, being ambitious in an artsy/theatrical way, immediately saw much more of a life for the musical than three nights at the '92.

Mailer and Stewart made it backstage and, amid the jubilant atmosphere, introduced themselves and made Miranda an offer that he chronicled years later in his Wesleyan commencement speech. "They said they loved it. They told that they were going to start a production company when they graduated and 'Will you call us when you graduate in two years because we want to help you bring *In the Heights* to New York.' I said 'That sounds awesome.' Then I went to the cast party and promptly forgot about the offer."

Mailer and Stewart were not all talk and no action. They immediately contacted recent Wesleyan graduate, Tommy Kail who at that point was in the very early stages of developing what would become Backhouse Productions. "John and Neil saw this early version of *In the Heights* and then they sent me this demo CD and the script," he told *Broadway Backstory*. "They said 'Hey when we start that company that we talked about that time at 3:30 in the morning, we should do this musical by this kid Lin Miranda."

Miranda put the script for *In the Heights* in a drawer where it would sit for two years. However,

Miranda would not be coasting through his last two years at Wesleyan. When he was offered the opportunity to study abroad during his junior year, he turned down the opportunity. "I have too many plays I agreed to work on," he related in his Wesleyan speech. "I am not throwing away my shot."

True to his word, Miranda's final two years at Wesleyan were marked by a number of theatrical endeavors post *In the Heights* as he continued to delve deeply into the nuts and bolts of forging a creative theatrical background. His senior thesis in particular, an essay about the lyrics of Alan Lerner, Oscar Hammerstein and Stephen Sondheim, was a masterful dissection that painstakingly compared and contrasted these master lyricists and their styles. Miranda would dissect this particular work in a conversation with the *Los Angeles Daily News.* "In learning how different those guys were and yet how masterful they were in their own way and then falling short of them, you find your own voice."

Miranda would write a total of four more musicals over the next two years, in his voice but, thematically, removed from *In the Heights*. He recalled two of the most expressive with *Hesherman.com*. "I wrote a jukebox musical called *Basket Case*. I wrote the book and it was all 90's songs. It was about a school shooting. I wrote another one called *On Borrowed Time* which was my senior thesis production, which if I have my way nobody will ever hear."

But on the night *On Borrowed Time* went before a live audience for the first and last time, some very important Wesleyan alums were in the audience. Mailer and Stewart, who had been as good as their word in keeping tabs on Miranda, had brought along two other former Wesleyan students, Thomas Kail and Anthony Veneziale to take a look at Miranda's latest creative effort. Needless to say, they shared Miranda's assessment of *On Borrowed Time* and were not bowled over by the experience.

They would meet with Miranda after the performance and after the obligatory congratulations on what they had just seen, they got down to the business of *In the Heights*. They reminded Miranda of their conversation two years earlier and now that he was about to graduate, they wanted him to know that they were still interested in doing something big with the musical. Miranda most likely did not remember their past conversation. But one thing was certain.

He went home that night and fished *In the Heights* out of that drawer. And took another look.

Chapter Eleven
Get a Job, Get a Life

Miranda graduated from Wesleyan University in 2002 with a Bachelor of Arts degree in Theater Arts. What that meant in the real world was that he had no job, no money and a pie-in-the-sky fantasy to hang his hopes and dreams on. In times like these, when he did not have an answer, he would usually turn to his family for advice.

But this time, Miranda took it upon himself to come up with an answer. Logic dictated that he needed enough money to put food on the table and some semblance of a roof over his head. But Miranda would easily contradict that notion with a need to have time to write, perform and make his dreams come true. He recalled his first stab at post college employment with *Hesherman.com.*

"When I was about to graduate from Wesleyan in 2002, I called my old high school mentor Dr. Herbert and said 'I have a BA in Theater Arts, can I come be a substitute at Hunter for a living?' He said 'I'll do you one better. We actually have a part-time English position.' So I taught seventh grade English my first year out of school."

Tommy Kail knew Miranda only in passing.

Already a senior at Wesleyan when *In the Heights* premiered at the school, Kail would acknowledge that he would occasionally butt heads with a competing Miranda production when it came to setting up lighting and scenery. But he was quite familiar with fellow students Mailer, Stewart and Veneziale and so he had gone along the night they had gone to see the less than spectacular *On Borrowed Time*.

But the buzz about *In the Heights* had been strong during the time that the group of aspiring theater alums had formed Backhouse Productions, a 50-seat performance space in the basement of the Drama Book Shop on West 40th Street in New York City. Watching *On Borrowed Time* that night, Kail and the other Backhouse people were more interested in waiting for the play to end so they could go backstage and reintroduce themselves to Miranda. "The four of us went up there [after the play was over] and sort of reintroduced ourselves to Lin," he told *Broadway Backstory*. "We had been communicating with him a little bit before then. That night it was more like 'Hey we did end up starting a theater company and would you like to come and work on the show you wrote two years ago and have probably not thought about very often since then?'"

The production company was anxious to get something going with Miranda and *In the Heights* but Kail and the others remained patient, waiting for the Spring of 2002 to approach Miranda about the possibility of workshopping *In the Heights* through Backhouse Productions and, hopefully, to the great white way. That first meeting of the minds took place at the Drama Bookstore and would be a marathon according to a *Washington Post* article. And one where ideas were falling like hailstones.

"We sat for five hours that first meeting," recalled Kail. "I felt like I had been looking for him my whole life and I didn't know." For his part, Miranda remembered that first meeting in equally positive tones. "I came into that meeting and Tommy is a tsunami, at that speed, hitting me with all this stuff. I would say that 50 percent of the ideas at that first meeting made it into the Broadway production."

What Miranda and Kail found during those early meetings was a very natural sense of simpatico and no small amount of trust on Lin's side. Kail related as how the vibe present in those early meetings in conversation with *Broadway Backstory* was of two very young men just trying to make sense of it all. "What I knew how to do was say 'let's look at those 20 minutes of the show, let's pull it apart and put it back together.' Lin had a lot of trust in what I was saying. He always just gave me the benefit of the doubt."

Between 2002 and 2003, Miranda was in the middle of a literal vortex. During the day, he was teaching seventh grade English at Hunter, an experience he would later describe as both challenging and positive. When not teaching, he could usually be found in meetings with Kail, Mailer and the rest of the Backhouse Production brain trust, going over ideas and dissecting Miranda's creation in an attempt to make *In the Heights* Broadway- ready and, most importantly, for a series of workshop productions in which investors would get a first look at *In the Heights* and decide if they wanted to invest in the production.

Then Miranda would go home and diligently write and rewrite what would finally be five separate drafts before everybody was satisfied that *In the Heights* was ready to show investors.

"I worked for about a year on making it into a full length musical and much more about the community," Miranda reflected in conversation with *Broadway Bullet.com*. "I wanted to create a piece of theater that also reflected the diversity of music in the neighborhood. I wanted to write musical theater music that I wouldn't be ashamed to blast in my car at full volume as I was driving down the street."

Unbeknownst to many to this day was the fact, between 2002 and 2003, a heretofore 'shadow producer,' an actor and childhood friend named David Moscow who was working with the Backhouse Productions group, was working below the radar to help attract both interest and investors in *In the Heights*.

Moscow chronicled his introduction to *In the Heights* during an interview with BroadwayWorld.com. Moscow recalled that his father, who was a business partner with Miranda's father Luis, called him up and said that Miranda had just graduated from Wesleyan and had 15 minutes of music he had written as part of his thesis. "Since I was in theater and putting on plays, I asked if I would listen to it and help. When I heard the music to *In the Heights* I thought 'Lock the doors! This shit is amazing.'"

Moscow was quick to incorporate his personal life and his professional connections to the advantage of Miranda and *In the Heights*. "We started putting money into it. I was dating the actress Kerry Washington then and so we ended up attaching her as a producer and actress. As we started to workshop it, the music went from the original 15 minutes to an hour. Kerry had just finished a Spike Lee project and so we brought him in to watch. He loved it and thought it might make a good movie. I had done a film with producer and friend Jill Furman so I invited her to one of the workshops and she fell in love with it, too."

Miranda was excited at the progress seemingly being made on behalf of *In the Heights*. But the day-to-day reality of making the rent was never far from his thoughts. His part-time teaching gig had been satisfying and, by year's end, the school was so happy with his work that they were prepared to offer him a full-time teaching position. Gratifying yes. A means of security, yes. But as he offered in an interview with *Hesheman.com*, he was torn at the prospect of gainful employment.

"They offered me a full-time teaching position at the end of the year and all I could see was a *Mr. Holland's Opus* life ahead of me." I said, 'I'll kick myself forever if I don't even try to work on this musical.'"

Searching for an answer, Miranda turned to his father Luis for the advice he knew would be forthcoming. He knew that there would be an answer because his father had always been conservative when it came to things like jobs and security and had, on several occasions when Miranda was growing up, nudged him in the direction of being a lawyer. So, Miranda was prepared for the 'cold hard facts' when he sat down for a heart-to-heart with his father.

"I asked him, 'What should I do?' he recalled in *Playbill.com*. "Should I keep teaching or should I just kind of sub and do gigs to pay the rent and really throw myself into writing fulltime?" In a letter Miranda recalled his father sending him, Miranda had his answer. "I really want to tell you to keep the job," his father said. "That's the smart, 'parent' thing to do. It makes no sense to leave your job to be a writer. But I have to tell you to do it."

Miranda had his answer.

"So I decided to basically quit teaching part-time to be a professional substitute which was much more precarious because you don't know if you'll make rent from month to month. But it is much less draining."

Consequently, Miranda would spend the next four years, floating in and out of classrooms, teaching elementary school Spanish, physics and science, more often than not providing just enough educational feedback to get his students and him through the day and to hold down the fort until the regular instructor returned.

In the Heights would continue in fits and starts through development hell, rewriting and expanding to its eventual two-act format. The music was constantly being restructured and refined to the point where everybody in the company was happy. Then came the tough part, the readings in front of potential investors who always seemed to have something to say. How tough those critiques from producers could be was chronicled in Miranda's speech to Wesleyan graduating students.

"Tommy Kail and I are meeting with a veteran theater producer. The big-deal theater producer has seen a reading and he is giving us his thoughts. We hang on his every word. This is a big deal theater producer and we are kids, desperate to get our show on. We are discussing the character of Nina Rosario, home from her first year at Stanford, the first in her family to go to college."

Thus far, things were looking up. The producer seemed interested in the finer points of Miranda's effort. He hadn't walked out in mid-reading. But Miranda would cringe as the conversation progressed.

"The big deal producer said, 'Now I know in your version Nina's coming home with a secret from her parents. She's lost her scholarship. The song is great. The actress is great. What I'm bumping up against, fellas, is that this doesn't feel high stakes enough. Scholarship? Big deal. What if she's pregnant? What if her boyfriend at school hit her? What if she got caught with drugs? It doesn't have to be any of those things. But you see what I'm getting at guys, a way to ramp up the stakes of your story."

The meeting concluded and the big-time producer left, leaving Miranda and Kail, sitting largely silent for a time before recapping the suggestions that were, intrinsically, repugnant to them but were enveloped by a certain reality. Creatively, the idea of the character Nina being pregnant or on drugs was counter to everything the pair had envisioned for *In the Heights*. But, as recalled by Miranda in his commencement speech, "But he wants to put our show up."

Miranda related that, "Tommy looks at me. That's not the story you want to tell and that's not the show I want to direct. There are ways to raise the stakes that are not that. We'll just keep working."

While continuing to rework and fine tune *In the Heights*, Miranda would find yet another outlet to flex his creative muscles when he co-founded the hip hop musical comedy troupe, Freestyle Love Supreme. For Miranda, Freestyle Love Supreme was a powerful conceit, the equivalent of jumping out of a plane without a parachute, a totally improvisational exercise in which the performers, which included a revolving cast of characters that, besides Miranda, included Christopher Jackson, Anthony Veneziale, Arthur Lewis, Chris Sullivan, James Monroe Inglehart and Bill Sherman, take their cues from the audience and turn them into fully realized musical numbers, literally on the spot. Freestyle Love Supreme would continue to perform and tour on a recurring basis over the years, and with money being tight, provided some semblance of irregular income.

Miranda acknowledged the total spontaneity and freedom Freestyle Love Supreme presented in conversation with *Broadway.com*. "Freestyle Love Supreme is based entirely off of audience suggestions. We have no idea what's going to happen. We run with what the audience throws at us."

It was a safe assumption that between 2003 and 2005, Miranda was not sleeping much. When not substitute teaching, he could often be spotted working on lyrics to *In the Heights* while riding the subway to and from work, which would often present an intimidating picture to fellow riders.

"I look like a crazy person on the subway when I'm writing," he related to *The New York Times*. "I sing and run around. I pace a lot."

And when substitute teaching was not always paying the rent, Miranda seemed forever in pursuit of very off-the-wall odd jobs. He found that MC'ing and providing the entertainment at bar mitzvahs could be lucrative and so it was with much chagrin that Miranda could be found center stage at very Jewish celebrations. "I was literally one of those guys who shows up in a black satin shirt and tries to get kids and old people to dance," he recalled to *The New York Times*. "It was bleak."

But while he continued to struggle to pay the rent, Miranda's creative fortunes were improving. Good word of mouth on *In the Heights* in the theatrical community soon brought author Quiara Alegria Hudes into the fold to write the theatrical book. An insightful and culturally aware writer, Hudes was quick to pick up on Miranda's desire for the play's sense of community and was soon able to turn *In the Heights* from the earlier love story into a much deeper examination of home, community and cultural identity. During this period, Alex Lacamore also came aboard as a steady handed music director to guide Miranda's many layers of music through the productions' theatrical moments. Equally important to the proceedings was the addition of choreographer Andy Blankenbuehler whose sense of intricacy and timing were brought into the production.

All that was now needed going into 2004 was an opportunity to get *In the Heights* before the public. The Eugene O'Neill Theater, the prestigious center of theatrical production in Connecticut, had become equally known for its National Music Theater Conference, which allowed little-known or experimental productions to be considered for active, limited run productions at the theater. Miranda and Hudes decided to take advantage of the theater's open submissions policy and submitted the story and the music of *In the Heights* for consideration. Both were happily surprised when their efforts were accepted for production.

What followed for Backhouse Productions and, particularly Miranda, was intense pre-production and preparation in which Miranda, in conjunction with director Kail and the other members of his fledgling team, wrote, cast, watched readings and made endless revisions to the story and music. There were tough choices to be made.

People who Miranda thought were ideal for certain roles would face uncertain futures in the play during revisions and, on at least one occasion, an actress had to be told that her character had been eliminated and, consequently, so had her part in the play. The irony being that the same actress was subsequently offered another part in *In the Heights* and would ultimately find out that character had been eliminated as well. Adding yet more challenges was that the requirements of The Eugene O' Neil Theater dictated that Miranda could not act in his own play.

Miranda revealed in *Broadway Backstory* the tough part for him was telling actors that their characters were not deemed necessary and that they were out of a job. "The character of Lincoln hung in there because he had good tunes. But then we realized that if we cut Lincoln and transferred some of his issues over to Nina, suddenly Nina became more complicated and we had all this room to tell all these other stories. So Lincoln died so the rest of us could live."

Miranda persisted in mounting his first real, professional level production of *In the Heights* and, by mid-summer, the nine-performance run (July 23-July 31) was about to open. Opening night for Miranda was hectic on any number of levels. Fear of failure and hope for success were uppermost in the young man's mind. As were last minute instructions and the placating of his cast's not unexpected mixture of excitement and nerves. The curtain went up on *In the Heights*. If Miranda said a little prayer and crossed his fingers, nobody would have been surprised.

The reviews were largely positive. Critics were seemingly getting the uniqueness of the story and the hip, up-to-the-moment nature of the music was strongly supported and appreciated as something new and excitingly different. Miranda and the others were ecstatic as the curtain rang down on July 31st. For Miranda, getting *In the Heights* out in the public eye was an important first step. But as he and the others in Backhouse Productions conferred in the days following the conclusion of the run, they were in agreement that there was still much more to do.

Producer Jill Furman acknowledged as much in looking back on the project with *Broadway Backstory*. "At this point, we didn't know what we were doing. We were either moving forward with the project or we were abandoning it. I don't think anyone thought we were abandoning it."

Chapter Twelve
Love and Robocalls

Miranda remembered Vanessa Adriana Nadal from his days at Hunter College High School. Sort of.

They would pass each other regularly in the hallway between classes and that was about it. Nadal was not a part of Miranda's crowd or any crowd for that matter. She was not looking to be popular. What Miranda would eventually discover was that she was super smart.

Nadal was on a fast educational track, heavy on math, science and the more cerebral subjects. She always seemed to have her nose in a book and was notorious for being ultra-prepared for exams. But what Miranda would discover was that there was a contrary side. She was into the music of the day, particularly hip hop and salsa and, as he would later discover, deeply entrenched in her Latino roots and culture.

Miranda was fresh off the success of *In the Heights* but still struggling to pay the rent when in the summer of 2005, he happened to be glancing through Facebook, seeing what fellow Hunter College High School graduates were up to, when he happened upon the profile of Nadal. He was both impressed and intrigued at what he read. After high school, Nadal went to the prestigious MIT. After graduation, Nadal went right to work as a scientist at the equally high-end Johnson & Johnson company where she was involved in various research and development projects. To say the least, Miranda was initially intimated by her intelligence as well as her beauty and might not have pursued her if it had not been for her musical interests that jumped off her Facebook page. With her interests in hip hop and salsa, Miranda felt he had a shot.

Freestyle Love Supreme had a show coming up. Miranda, summoning up no small amount of courage, sent Nadal an instant message inviting her to the show. No one was more surprised than Miranda when she showed up. After the performance, Nadal joined Miranda for drinks. How the evening went depended on who one talked to according to *The New York Times*.

"It was a huge group so he didn't talk to me the whole night," recalled Nadal. "I didn't think he was interested in me." For his part, Miranda painted a different picture. "If she had just paid attention, she would have known from my darting furtive glances. But I was so shy I asked a friend of mine to get her phone number for me."

Some weeks later, Miranda called Nadal and invited her to another Freestyle Love Supreme performance. Miranda knew she was in the audience and may well have been inspired to give an electrifying performance. At least that's the way Nadal perceived it. "When he came onstage, I thought 'I really like this guy. He was up there freestyling and weaving rhymes together. It was (really) impressive."

After the performance, Nadal was once again part of an after-party crowd that consisted primarily of Miranda's friends, a literal living tapestry of rappers, artists and break dancers. Far from being a shrinking violet in the face of Miranda's 'out there friends, he marveled at how easily Nadal mixed and mingled with his people. Eventually the party broke up and everybody drifted away, except for Nadal and Miranda. At one point, Nadal acknowledged that the hustle and bustle of the big city reminded her of a scene from her favorite video game, *Grand Theft Auto* which, coincidentally, was his favorite game as well.

Miranda instantly discovered his 'cool' as he related to *The New York Times*. "I very coolly said 'All right, you're going to come over to my house tonight and we're going to play *Grand Theft Auto*, watch the Jay-Z movie and listen to Marc Anthony."

What else transpired that night is left to the imagination but it was safe to say that, by the next morning, Nadal and Miranda were head over heels for each other. In a matter of days, they had mutually agreed to call each other boyfriend and girlfriend. Things moved pretty fast at that point. They would exchange apartment keys and, given their respective schedules, Nadal would often arrive home at her apartment to find Miranda crouched in a corner, composing on his keyboard. Nadal grew to understand Miranda's quirks as did he hers.

The couple made an immediate effort to integrate their families and friends into this new stage in their lives. Nadal recalled in *The New York Times* that "He made a concerted effort to introduce me to every person who was important to him, which showed me I was important. He gets me in a way that no one else does. I'm a scientist at heart. I try very hard not to let my emotions cloud my judgments and he'll see right through that and see what I was feeling."

By 2006, Miranda, now happily involved and truly in love, remained in a never-ending cycle of creative poverty and the maddening round of freelance jobs designed to pay the rent while working and reworking the latest version of *In the Heights*. Adding to the blur of activity was the constant but polite nattering of his father, Luis, that it might be time to go to law school, reminding him that noted actor Ruben Blades had obtained a law degree. But when Miranda made it plain that his future plans did not include a law degree but, rather, the Broadway stage, Luis finally took the hint and offered his son a job instead.

The elder Miranda had long ago established a thriving political consulting group called the Mir Ram Group whose purpose was to guide and mold the image of mainly New York political candidates. Which often translated into creating radio and television ads and the necessity for background music. Which led, in turn, to Luis hiring his son to create musical jingles for his political clients' ads. Luis struck an altruistic tone on the subject when he told *The New York Times* "The work with me allowed him to sort of dedicate his life to art." But in the same interview, he would admit that he hired his son because he charged less than other composers and he needed the work.

Miranda would supply the musical backing to ads for the likes of Al Sharpton, Fernando Ferrer, the infamous Eliot Spitzer, H. Carl McCall and David S.

Yassky. Miranda would recall that doing political jingles, in which his musical backing would play out under a montage of the candidate doing seemingly important things and meeting the public, was not the most creatively challenging or inspired work.

"He [my dad] would say something like 'I need 30 seconds of some jazz for a Sharpton spot that's going to be on radio station WBLS or I need some bright salsa for a Fernando Ferrer campaign commercial," he explained in a *National Public Radio* commercial. "I wrote music for Eliot Spitzer, before we knew what we knew about him, when he was running for governor and I wrote for Carl McCall and whatever Democrat was running or my dad was working with. I was writing the campaign music. I liked writing the negative ads more. I just kind of hit the synthesizer. Politician X voted against da da da and then it would end with some bright salsa music and vote Politician Y."

Miranda, who likened what he was doing to scoring a movie, did get one chance to flex his hip hop muscles when his father asked him to write a rap for a robocall that the rapper Fat Joe was expected to make for a candidate's mayoral campaign. What Miranda would remember of the exercise in political flackery was not much. "I remember the hook was 'Freddy Ready, he recalled to *The New York Times*. "That's about all I remember from it.

"I don't think it ever got used."

Chapter Thirteen
Off the Grid

Shortly after the conclusion of the Eugene O'Neill Theater run of *In the Heights*, Miranda, Kail and just about every member of the production went back to their day jobs. Not surprisingly, *In the Heights* had been a smashing creative success. Also not surprising, the venture had made little if any money and so, in a real world sense, *In the Heights* was back to square one. To go any further meant they needed financial backers.

Enter a couple of angels named Kevin McCollum and Jeffrey Seller. McCollum and Seller had been legends in the East Coast theater community for some years, having produced and backed countless Broadway hits including *Rent*, *Private Lives* and *High Fidelity*. As fate would have it, the pair had recently renovated a parking lot and had built a theater that they christened 37 Arts. The 37 Arts was scaled at 499 seats, an ideal place for smaller productions and, in the case of *In the Heights*, to workshop the play to interested investors.

McCollum liked the idea of shepherding a little known effort by unknown creatives and, after initial conversations and hearing and seeing elements of the completed production to that point, agreed to put on a series of three workshop productions with an eye toward getting enough front money to take a shot Off Broadway. The workshop presentations at 37 Arts were successful in getting enough seed money (reportedly in the neighborhood of $2.5 million) to begin seriously thinking about taking *In the Heights* off Broadway.

It had been a tradition that most shows going the Off Broadway route would do their early performances out of the big city, the better to work out any production kinks away from the New York and Los Angeles critics who could kill a show, literally in the womb, with an early negative review. But the reasoning was that since *In the Heights* was very much an urban, New York kind of story, it made sense that their attempt at Off Broadway should be literally done in the town that spawned it. And rather then searching for another theater for the launch, it made sense to keep the production in the by-now manageable confines of 37 Arts.

For Miranda, the polishing and fine-tuning continued literally up to opening night. Songs were reevaluated and reconfigured, as were characters and roles which led to *In the Heights'* unheralded happy ending when actress/singer Doreen Montalvo, who had been dismissed from the production a year earlier, was brought back in a secondary role that, nevertheless, would prove a potent singing and acting opportunity.

Marketing *In the Heights* would be a whole other matter. Competition for the theater-going audience dollar was extremely fierce even at the Off Broadway level. It was decided that word of mouth and scaled ticket prices would be the way to build momentum and a following targeting the very audience represented in *In the Heights*--the young, hip and low income. A no comps ticket policy was the first order of the day which, initially frustrated several notable Broadway bigwigs' attempts to get free tickets. But in its place was a unique sliding ticket pricing. The first week tickets were only $20, the second week $30, the fourth week $40 up to a price of $65 from that point on.

In the Heights would open February 8, 2007 and would run 26 weeks to its final curtain call on July 15, 2007. The run would total 33 preview performances and 182 regular performances. For Miranda, the run of *In the Heights* would be an often-grueling test. As one of the lead actors in the production, Miranda was constantly on creative high alert for what did and did not work in his own performance as well as the other cast members. Any free time, and truth be known, there was little of that, would find him in disguise in the audience during the occasional show in which his understudy took over to gauge the audience's feedback to the show in live time.

Despite the relatively small seating capacity of 37 Arts, word of mouth was quickly spreading. The audience was regularly running between 250 and 400 people a performance. The show was taking in just enough money to pay people on a weekly basis and, although *In the Heights* would never recoup its investment during its Off Broadway run, the buzz was growing thanks to good word of mouth and the largely positive reviews from some highly influential corners.

Theater Mania rang in with a review that reported, "The sensational new musical *In the Heights* may not please everyone but plenty of people are going to leave Off Broadway's 37 Arts Theater with words like 'exuberant' and 'exciting' coming out of their mouths." *New York Magazine* chimed in with,

"The most obvious of this show's many virtues is that it doesn't sound like the half-assed pseudo pop that clutters up Broadway. Miranda's score is rich and kaleidoscopic. The dancers feel like they really might have come off the street." And in a review that struck a personal note with Miranda, *The New York Times* offered, "A singular new sensation, Lin-Manuel Miranda, commanded the spotlight as if he were born in the wings. A tuneful score enlivened by dancing rhythms, zesty choreography that seems to put invisible wings on the young cast's neon-colored sneakers and a stage stocked with appealing actors."

Before its official Off Broadway run was over, *In the Heights* and its fledgling creator were already the feel-good story of the East Coast theater elite with a literal flood of awards coming its way. The Outer Critics Circle Award honored the musical for Outstanding Musical and Outstanding Choreography. The prestigious Lucille Lortel Award honored the musical with awards for Outstanding Musical and Outstanding Choreography. The equally creditable Drama Desk Awards presented *In the Heights* with Outstanding Ensemble Performance and Outstanding Choreography while The Obie Award was presented to Miranda and company for Outstanding Music and Lyrics. For his part, Miranda was the recipient of individual honors by the Equity Clarence Derwent organization and Theater World.

But by that time, *In the Heights* was already literally dancing in the streets when the producers called the cast and crew together to announce that they were taking *In the Heights* that all-important next step forward.

The show was going to Broadway.

Chapter Fourteen
The High Life

Everyone was in agreement that the Richard Rodgers Theater would be the ideal venue to bring *In the Heights* to the bright lights of Broadway. Owing to scheduling and the popularity of the theater, it would be at least six months before it would be available. Which was fine because, a lot needed to be done to bring *In the Heights* to the next level of professional presentation.

The script was revised and a detailed advertising campaign was planned out. A television commercial was shot. Miranda took a long, hard look at the music of *In the Heights* and, ever the perfectionist, decided to eliminate three of the Off Broadway songs and wrote three new ones. In a conversation with *Vulture.com*, Miranda related some of the changes in taking *In the Heights* to that next step. "We've added four more people to the mix, it's a bigger ensemble and more swings. Off Broadway, if more than three people were sick, we'd have to do a cut show. Now we have understudies. Off Broadway, I used my own belt for my own pants. Now I have a belt for every pair of pants in the show, none of which are mine."

As busy as he was now and as successful as the Off Broadway production had been, Miranda was still living at poverty level. He would continue to do substitute teaching as it became available but, during this period, would also dip his toe into some very slight acting work in television and films and some just plain goofing off.

Miranda can be seen very briefly in a 2007 sixth season *The Sopranos* episode entitled "Remember" when as a bellman pushing a cart, Miranda moves quickly in and out of frame. Miranda went uncredited and did it for laughs and the bucks. But a bit of an urban myth has grown up around the appearance as he was reportedly credited as 'that fuckin' guy.' Check those credits closely. Shortly before *In the Heights* moved to Broadway, Miranda and his director buddy Kail appeared in the *Sex in The City Movie* as two guys moving a couch. Again, Miranda went uncredited and their 30 seconds of screen time resulted in a snippet of dialogue that consisted of the word 'yeah.' And although they would not actually air for another year, Miranda took time off in 2008 to do guest starring turns in the children's series *Sesame Street* and *The Electric Company*. In the former, he portrayed Freddy Flapman in the episode "Frankly It's A Habitat" while the latter saw him playing the character of Mario in the episode "One Bad Apple." Never one to let writer's block dissuade him, Miranda took a temporary creative dip to exercise his inner musical roots in a hilarious, extremely theatrical romp through a park to the tune of *High School Musical 2's* Bet On It.

The early success of *In the Heights* had made Miranda the next big thing on Broadway and the result was that he now had entryway and guidance from some of the biggest names in theater who were anxious to make his acquaintance. A long-standing friendship with composer Stephen Sondheim that dated from an early meeting when the legendary composer spoke at Miranda's high school had since flowered into a full-blown unofficial mentorship in which Miranda would regularly send Sondheim unfinished work for him to critique. Songwriter Stephen Schwartz had also become someone Miranda could regularly bounce ideas off of and well-known composer John Kander, after meeting Miranda after attending an Off Broadway performance of *In the Heights*, also became a close, personal friend. In a *New York Times* conversation, Kander gushed that, "Lin is a boy genius. What Lin is is a refreshing and contemporary synthesis of everything he's known before."

The respect was mutual as Miranda offered in *Vulture.com*. "John Kander's become a really good friend in this process and has become a big champion of the show. I got to meet Arthur Laurents and Stephen Flaherty who wrote *Ragtime* and Jeanine Tesori who composed *Thoroughly Modern Millie*. I was meeting all my heroes."

But all the schmoozing and bit acting roles aside, Miranda's primary occupation in the months leading up to *In the Heights'* Broadway debut was getting his creative baby ready for its birth. Miranda continued to be exacting to a fault. He was instinctive in preparing the finished product. If there was even a hint that a song or production number did not work, he went immediately and willingly back to the drawing board. There were long days and nights of rehearsal as the cast rounded into their roles and how important it would be to all fit together. Miranda easily saw *In the Heights* a hundred times in its rehearsal stage.

In his mind it was more like a million. The question of whether *In the Heights* would fly or flop on Broadway would soon be answered.

Previews began on February 14, 2008. As always, there would be last minute fine-tuning and timing issues to be dealt with but everybody connected to the production felt everything was in hand in the days leading up to their Broadway debut on March 8, 2008. For Miranda, the curtain would officially rise and the fantasy ride would begin.

Early reviews were by and large very good, with the occasional jab at the fact that *In the Heights* did not address the cliché *West Side Story* style of gang violence and crime in the Latino community. Miranda knew that those critiques were coming and, during endless rounds of press interviews tied to *In the Heights'* opening, he had a ready response. "It was jarring for people who haven't spent time in Washington Heights to not see scenes like the one in *Shaft*, where the drug deal takes place In the Heights," he explained to *Vulture.com*. "But, if I had tried to put that in, I wouldn't have been honest with my experience there. That stuff existed but it wasn't central to my upbringing."

Fortunately, those would be only minor bumps on the critical landscape amid a wash of ecstatic and often gushing reviews. *The New York Times* offered, "When the music erupts in one of its expressions of collective joy, the energy it gives off could light up the George Washington Bridge for a year or two." *The Cleveland Plain Dealer* reported, "The exciting set and choreography held my interest in the storyline." *Variety's* review would be particularly heartfelt to

Miranda when it stated, "The depth of feeling, together with the wit of Miranda's lyrics, the playful dexterity of his rhymes, his dynamic score and a bunch of truly winning performances make the show an uncalculated charmer."

Perhaps more important than the reviews, was the fact that *In the Heights* was succeeding across cultural, racial and generational lines. It would not be uncommon during what would be the 29 preview performances and 1,184 regular performances to see young Latino hipsters sitting next to a middle-aged white couple. That the show was a critical and creative success went without saying. That it could succeed in the often harsh financial aspect of Broadway theater would be the capper on a magical time when, on January 9, 2008, the production had earned back its estimated $10 million investment in 10 months and was now officially in the black.

And with that kind of success, the perks began flooding in. To wit: The original cast recording of *In the Heights* was released on June 3, 2008 and would go on to capture a Grammy Award for Best Musical Show Album. *In the Heights* would soon get that rarest of honors, a nomination for the Pulitzer Prize for Best Drama. Needless to say, the movie world was quick to jump on the theatrical success of *In the Heights*. Universal Pictures would step up to the plate in November 2008, when it was announced that they would adapt the musical to the big screen, with Miranda starring and noted choreographer Kenny Ortega directing, for release in 2011. Unfortunately, owing to the vagaries of Hollywood, that deal would ultimately fall through.

On a happier note, *In the Heights* became the subject of a PBS television documentary, in May 2009, when the Public Broadcasting System, as part of their Great Performances series, aired a documentary entitled *In the Heights: Chasing Broadway Dreams* which chronicled Miranda and his production company's two year odyssey from its Off Broadway premiere to the triumph of the 2008 Tony Awards. *In the Heights* had, indeed, captured the hearts and minds of the theater-going world and the result had been a massive nod from the Tony Awards committee, to the tune of 13 nominations, the most of any nominated production that year.

Radio City Music Hall was ground zero for the Tony Awards and for the cast of *In the Heights* it would not be leisurely. That afternoon a matinee was presented with polish. Then it was a quick limo ride over to the ceremonies where Miranda and the cast did the red carpet walk, then it was to the three rows at the back of the orchestra where the cast held hands and nervously speculated on what was to come that night. The consensus among critics was that *In the Heights* would be a big winner that night.

And for Miranda, who reflected on those memories in *Broadway Backstory*, it was all too much giddy emotion. "Every moment of that day was surreal. Our lives changed before the main section of the Tony's went on television when the show won Tony's for Best Orchestration and Best Choreography."

Adding to the electricity of the night, the *In the Heights* cast would also be doing a musical number live in prime time entitled "96,000." The conceit of that moment was that while the majority of Tony night performances were led by one individual singer, "96,000" would be presented as it was every night on the stage, a true ensemble moment with elements of song and dance forming a non-stop wall of sound and movement that left the audience breathless.

And paved the way for Miranda and *In the Heights* to take the Tony for the Best Original Score. As the night's festivities moved to their conclusion, the one award on everybody's mind throughout the evening was about to be unveiled... Best Musical. It was a moment that Miranda had dreamed of and, like everything in his life and career to that point, he had taken seriously.

"I practiced [my acceptance speech] in the shower but never wrote it down," he told *Broadway Backstory*. "I just had a couple of couplets in my head that I had in the chamber if I won. It would be easier for me to say it and make it rhyme then to get all emotional and make it blubbery. I had those couplets already in my head."

And Miranda would recall the moment when *In the Heights* was announced as Best Musical. "Half of them [the couplets] flew out the window. You can actually see the moment when it leaves my head. Because that's when the cast started screaming. And that's when some receptor in my brain said 'this is real, this is real.' This is not you in a mirror with a comb...

..."This is real."

Chapter Fifteen
So Now What?

By January 2009, Miranda was beginning to take some nights off. Going into the home stretch of its year-long plus run, *In the Heights* could, more often than not, run itself. But Miranda could not stay away too long and so it was that in late January, he returned to the stage as the character Usnavi in what would be the final 19 Broadway performances of *In the Heights*. As much of a realist as Miranda had become during the previous couple of years piloting his creations' fortunes, one could not forgive him for waxing sentimental as he stood center stage for the final curtain call on February 15, 2009.

"It was unreal," Miranda told an *AARP* interviewer. "I came out with a five minute standing ovation. Having done the show for a year, you learn to do the show so you can do it safely eight shows a week. But the feeling that night was that I don't have another one coming and so we've all got to leave it all on the stage tonight."

Miranda immediately went into decompression mode. If you were looking for him during the first week after the Broadway closing of *In the Heights*, the chances are you would not find him...unless you happened to be passing through Las Vegas. "I took a page out of the play and took my *abuelita* (grandmother) to Vegas for a couple of days which was fantastic," he fondly recalled to *AARP*. "We went to the Bellagio for a couple of days and I wheeled her around to every slot machine we could find. We had a great time."

But Miranda's thoughts were never far from the next project that would challenge him and what he was finding, post-*In the Heights*, was that many of the brighter lights in the theater community were coming to him for help. One of the first to send up a creative flare was good friend, composer/lyricist and director Stephen Schwartz who was mounting a new adaptation of the Stud's Terkel book *Working*.

Working had a checkered history in its previous attempts to translate from book to theater, often enticing but, just as often flawed. Schwartz's reboot was crying out for some new music and nobody was hotter at the moment than Miranda. Riding high from his Tony victories, Miranda seemed excited at the prospect of writing two songs for somebody else's production and he was diligent in researching the concept of working, going so far as to interview people at McDonalds to get a sense of the working life at what most perceived as the paycheck to paycheck life.

Miranda acknowledged the process of creating *Working* songs with *AARP*. "One of my songs ["Delivery"] is about doing delivery for a fast food chain which was actually my first job as a kid. For the other song ["A Very Good Day"] we really wanted to write a new song about what the immigrant working experience is like in this country. For that song I interviewed several day care workers and babysitters and wrote the song about how every immigrant group gets their foot in the door by doing the job nobody else wants to do."

While contributing original songs to *Working* was a welcome challenge, Miranda was literally over the moon when director Arthur Laurents came to him with an extremely progressive request surrounding a newly mounted revival of *West Side Story*. "He [Laurents] had a very audacious idea for this revival," Miranda recalled in *AARP*. "He said 'I want the Sharks to talk to each other in Spanish when they're with each other and to sing in Spanish when they feel like singing to each other.' He said 'Do you think you can do that?' And I said "I think I was born to do that.' "

The opportunity struck at the very core of Miranda's life long sense of cultural equality and representation for Latinos. He was determined to use this opportunity to the max in presenting a *West Side Story* for a new generation. But before he could do that, he still needed the blessing of the man who was with *West Side Story* from its inception. Stephen Sondheim.

"We met a couple of times," Miranda told *AARP*. "He was very generous about allowing me to find whatever language I needed to express the sentiments of the songs. What he was adamant about was the structure and rhyme. With a lot of Spanish language translations, the rhyme is the first thing that is sacrificed so that the lyrics can make sense in Spanish. So I really tried to strike a balance between honoring the original lyric structure and continuing to have it make sense and be just as witty and effortless in Spanish as it is in its own amazing English lyrics."

This 'modern' version of *West Side Story* would ultimately have a solid but not spectacular run, owing to the perceived notion, mainly proffered by the production's investor and, much more delicately by the producers, that the level of Spanish in the production was confusing theater goers and softening the impact of the overall production. After some spirited back and forth, a compromise was reached as the amount of Spanish was cut back but not completely eliminated. Miranda felt like the experiment had been a success and learned a valuable lesson about the impact that the moneymen of the theater world can have on the creative effort.

"I was satisfied," Miranda told *AARP*. "Sondheim was satisfied and my dad was satisfied. Those were my two benchmarks."

In October of 2009, Miranda was involved in prepping the first national tour of *In the Heights*. Although he would not be starring in the role of Usnavi, he would occasionally pop in and out of the tour to play Usnavi as well as to get a first hand view of how *In the Heights* was doing on a national level. Part of Miranda relished those moments to relive his theatrical breakthrough. But in the wake of his Tony Awards triumph, his creative mind was constantly wondering and new opportunities and challenges seemed around every corner.

One such call came in the guise of the television series *House's* executive producer. As it turns out, she was a fan of *In the Heights* and the show's writers were working on a character with Miranda in mind, a bipolar hip hop artist named Juan 'Alvie' Alvarez who is House's roommate in a psych ward. Miranda was intrigued. It also did not hurt that he was a fan of the show. He immediately cleared his schedule and was off to Los Angeles.

The one shot appearance in the episode "Broken" would actually turn into a second episode entitled "Baggage'" The chemistry between Miranda and Hugh Lurie was excellent in front of the camera as their character eccentricities were a perfect fit according to Miranda in *Playbill.com.* "The best way of putting it is that I play Tigger to his Eeyore."

It was safe to say that Miranda, now christened by the press as the hot new composer on the scene, was being bombarded with ideas that would spark his interest. Miranda was being careful and weighed every offer. But with his involvement in a now national tour of *In the Heights* taking up much of his time, getting him to commit to much of anything at that point was a tough challenge…even to those in his immediate circle.

Such was the case one night during the Broadway run of *In the Heights* when Miranda was approached by his choreographer Andy Blankenbuehler with the idea of bringing a ten-year old and largely disposable movie to Broadway as a musical. The movie was *Bring It On*, a 2000 battle of the cheerleaders epic that had succeeded as a cult film with enough support to spawn four sequels. Miranda dutifully listened as Blankenbuehler gave his pitch. Miranda offered *Black Book.com* that he remembered *Bring It On*. "I was in college. It was 2000 and I remembered thinking 'Wow! This is a really funny movie.' But, initially, Miranda was not moved.

"When he gave me the pitch, I kind of shrugged," he told *The Orange County Register*. "I had fond memories of the original movie but that was about all. But I slept on it and the thought of Andy choreographing a bunch of cheerleaders was just too good to resist."

It also did not hurt his decision that Tom Kitt, Pulitzer Prize-winning composer for the musical *Next To Normal* and Amanda Green, a respected lyricist thanks to a litany of musical contributions that included the multi-award winning musical *High Fidelity*, were interested and circling the fledgling project. Also sweetening the creative pot was the book writer Jeff Witty who, smartly, took only the movie title and cheerleader concept from the source material and had fashioned a truly smart high school storyline that borrowed liberally from more adult themes. But what sold Miranda, emotionally, on the concept was that, while stylistically updated with a musical mixture of pop and hip hop, *Bring It On: The Musical* would never stray far from classic high school tropes.

Miranda said as much in a conversation with *Playbill.com* when he cut to the core of high school as the perfect jumping off point. "It [high school] is just when you feel the most! You have the most feelings per second. You're bursting with hormones and everything is life or death."

Miranda, Kitt and Green soon settled into the writing process for *Bring It On: The Musical*. Many observers of those early days must have crossed their fingers at how three superior talents would get along. Some, privately, predicted that inherent egos might make for a bumpy ride. Happily, the writing process for *Bring It On: The Musical* would be an object lesson in just how well Miranda was able to get along with others according to memories supplied by Kitt and Green to *Playbill.com*.

Kitt distilled the writing process between Miranda and himself as an organic give and take. "I would come in and hear a piece of music that Lin brought in and it would just blow me away. I would become inspired for the other moments of the show. It just felt like we would one up each other, and not in the sense of being competitive, but, literally, lifting each other up by our own participation in the process."

For Green's part, she recalled constantly marveling at what the three contributors brought to the table. "It was fun learning how themes from one of Lin's songs could work, in a later moment, in one of Tom's songs. It was definitely up for grabs."

Bring It On: The Musical had a fairly leisurely gestation process which allowed for the trio of composers to fine tune the compositions to fit the action-packed, frenetic pace of the musical. Which was fine with Miranda.

"The work on *Bring It On* is never finished," he told *Playbill.com* with no small sense of irony. "There's always something that could be a little sharper...a little better."

Chapter Sixteen
Discovering Hamilton

The Broadway run of *In the Heights* was just concluding. The national touring company for *In the Heights* was just gearing up. To say that Miranda was in need of a break was an understatement. Which was why he decided to take some alone time with his then-girlfriend Nadal and travel to Mexico for a bit of rest and relaxation.

Which if you believe the popular story is where Miranda discovered Hamilton. A notion that was very Miranda like, a bit spontaneous, a bit theatrical and seemed to fit his modus operandi of rampant creativity with a DIY bent. But as it turned out, the popular story was not necessarily the whole story. Whatever story one chooses to believe, the reality is consistent and the jumping off point was a wildly groundbreaking biography of Hamilton by noted author and historian Ron Chernow.

Chernow had long since established a reputation as a biographer of historical figures that transcended a mere scholarly audience to a wider reaching, layman's and, lest we consider it, a more mainstream group of readers on the strength of literate and accessible looks at the lives of J.P. Morgan, John D. Rockefeller, The Warburgs and, some years later, Ulysses S. Grant. But it would remain until the 2004 publication of *Hamilton* to truly cement his reputation and destroy the myths of dry, scholarly works. *Hamilton*, clocking in at 832 pages and a hefty 2.8 pounds, touched all the critical bases. It was deep in research, probing in its overall approach and joyously thick in its critical eye, insightful reality and, ultimately, a cutting respect for a life well lived as history unfolded.

It seemed that Hamilton was rife with possibilities for somebody like Miranda. And according to author/critic and close confidant of Miranda, Jeremy McCarter, the process of discovering Hamilton started a bit earlier than the Mexico vacation as he offered in the book *Hamilton: The Revolution* and later excerpted by *Vox.com*.

"Our late night conversations about a hip hop version of Hamilton's life happened a week before he started on that trip. After much baffled pouring over of emails, we realized he must have already read a few chapters as soon as he bought the book and that was enough for him to come up with the idea and even a title: *The Hamilton Mixtape*."

But it would take that trip to Mexico where, in between frolicking on the beaches and sightseeing with Vanessa, he would immerse himself in the book and the much deeper mythos of Hamilton and, in the process, discover an unexpected attraction to everything about him," he told *The Guardian* "What I knew about Hamilton prior to picking up that book was that he was the dead white guy on the $10 bill. I had written about him in high school. I knew his son had died in a duel and that he had died in a duel. I think that's what took the book off the shelf and into my hand."

But Miranda would eventually read the book from cover to cover and discover modern parallels. "In a way he was like a hip hop artist," he told *The Guardian*. "I began to see parallels in my own life and in the life of my father. I just recognized the guy."

By the time he completed the book, Miranda suddenly found himself wrapped up in a passion project, as he would reflect in *Playbill.com*. "Something about it just grabbed me. As I read it, I realized that Hamilton's whole life was about the power of words and that wouldn't it be great to hear a hip hop album about how we created this country."

All enthusiasm aside, Miranda, once the initial rush of obsession subsided, was tentative about how to approach this newfound passion. "I was like 'this is an album, no this is a show,' he told *Vogue*. "How has no one done this? So I Googled Alexander Hamilton: Hip Hop Musical and I expected to see that somebody had already done it. But no [they had not]. So I got to work."

Vanessa, most certainly, could sense that her boyfriend was, emotionally and creatively, just a bit distracted and that, for the remainder of their time in Mexico, what had been an idyllic sojourn away from the hustle and bustle of their busy lives, she would be sharing her time with two men. Miranda and Hamilton. In a conversation with *The Huffington Post*, Miranda knew that playtime was suddenly giving way to work. "When I picked up Ron Chernow's biography, I was at a resort in Mexico on my first vacation from *In the Heights* in seven years. The moment my brain got a moment's rest, Hamilton walked into it."

Miranda was so enthralled and enraptured by *Hamilton* that he made it his mission, upon returning to the states to track down its author. Chernow, in conversation with *Newsweek*, recalled how Miranda would come calling. "Back in the fall of 2008, I ran into a friend in the neighborhood whose daughter had gone to Wesleyan with Lin-Manuel Miranda. He started by telling me, 'This hip hop artist,' as he referred to Lin, had read my Hamilton book, it had made this enormous impression on him and he was excited to find out if he could meet me."

Using his friend as an intermediary, Chernow agreed to go to a Sunday matinee of *In the Heights*. The author was instantly struck by the power of the show and, in particular, the music. Backstage after the performance, Chernow found an excited yet respectful Miranda who immediately told the author what he had in mind. Which would be either a concept album on the life of Alexander Hamilton or, if it went according to plan, his second Broadway musical.

"I could tell from that very first conversation with Lin that he wanted to do a very serious, dramatic rendering," he told *Newsweek*. "I could see that he wanted to capture Hamilton in the way that I had in the book."

Admittedly, Chernow, as he offered in *The New York Times*, was naïve to the ways of hip hop and so he asked Miranda if hip hop could be the vehicle to tell such a rich and complex story. "He said 'Ron, I'm going to educate you.' He pointed out how dense, rapid lyrics could pack an enormous amount of information into songs."

By the end of that first meeting, Chernow, creatively, had drank the Kool Aid, and saw the possibilities of his book being taken into heretofore unimagined realms. Which is why he readily accepted Miranda's offer to be his creative consultant on the project. Miranda's reason for asking for Chernow's help was to the point as he opined in *The New York Times*.

"I want the historians to take this seriously."

Chernow and Miranda agreed to work together and then went their separate ways. Until some months later. Miranda had been busy and the result was something he wanted Chernow to hear. "Three months after that first meeting, Lin asked me if he could come over and sing something for me," he recalled in conversation with *The New York Times*. "He sat on my living room couch, began to snap his fingers and then sang the opening song of what would become *Hamilton*. When he finished he asked me what I thought? I told him 'I think that's the most astonishing thing I've ever heard in my entire life.' He had accurately condensed the first 40 pages of my book into a four-minute song."

The song in question, which went by the working title "Ten Dolla Founding Father" in its embryonic stage, would be the jumping off point for Miranda. Every free moment would be spent refining it and slowly moving on to tell the rest of the story. At this point, Miranda was primarily focused on turning his obsession with Hamilton into the oft-mentioned hip hop album. But the thought that a combination of history and hip hop might just work on the stage was never far from his thoughts. A glimmer of what might show promise for the latter came his way when in April of 2009, Miranda received an offer to perform that he could not refuse.

President Barack Obama, then less than a year

into what would be his first term as the de facto leader of the free world, and his First Lady Michelle, were considered super progressive in their thoughts and attitudes, especially when it came to embracing diversity. In line with that, they had come up with the idea of a coming out party of sorts at The White House, billed as An Evening of Poetry, Music and The Spoken Word depicting various interpretations of the American Experience. The event would have national and cultural implications and would be covered by a myriad of mainstream and alternative press that included *The Los Angeles Times*, *CBS News*, *The New Yorker* and *Paste Magazine*.

Miranda would later disclose to *CBS News* that he was honored to be invited but, as the May 12, 2009 performance loomed closer, he was also scared to death. "I was a terrified young Puerto Rican man. I mean there was the leader of the free world, the newly elected leader of the free world, his entire family, Vice President Joe Biden."

Miranda would also discover that he would be in the company of super star quality co-performers, the likes of jazz bassist and vocalist Esperanza Spalding and legendary actor James Earl Jones. "Yeah, I was nervous," he related to *Paste Magazine*. "You know that any day that starts with a van ride to The White House with James Earl Jones is a surreal day to begin with."

Miranda had been advised that any selection from *In the Heights* would be a welcome addition to the program. But Miranda had other ideas and he was about to take a risk. Rather than do a piece from *In the Heights*, he nervously stepped before the mic and addressed the President and the other assembled dignitaries.

"I'm actually working on a hip hop album. It's a concept album about the life of someone I think embodies hip hop, Treasury Secretary Alexander Hamilton."

There was some mild laughter and applause. Miranda launched into his rap, a rip-roaring, raw lyrical rush of jagged pictures of Hamilton's early life, the good and the bad. In his gut, Miranda was praying that the well-heeled audience would be drawn to the song and not repelled by it. Miranda, gyrating through his angst-ridden diatribe that, at its core, was telling a deeply felt, emotional look at the trials and tribulations of a boy who would grow up to be one of America's influential figures, was scared to death even as he was doing his thing.

"At one point [during his performance] I looked out into the audience and saw Obama turn to Michelle and mouth the words 'this is great,'" he related to *Paste*. "At that point, I was so nervous I couldn't look at them for the rest of the performance."

Miranda finished his performance and stared out into the audience. He was greeted with thunderous applause by some of the most politically inclined people in America. Later that night he would gratefully accept congratulations from people of influence who thought they knew Hamilton but had suddenly discovered something new. Miranda smiled a broad, boyish smile.

The first public performance of *Hamilton* was a success. But the last thing on Miranda's mind was that his debut at The White House would quickly turn into an internet sensation. His first *Hamilton* performance immediately went viral, inspiring countless parodies, video covers, college and high school performances of the song and an untold number of original songs about Hamilton. The bottom line in this sudden adulation was that fans were clamoring for the rest of *The Hamilton Mixtape*.

Among those who would be introduced to the potential for *Hamilton*, based on that one song performed before the President of The United States, was Oskar Eustis who had been the artistic director of The Public Theater since 2005. In May 2009, shortly after the video of Miranda's performance had gone viral, Eustis received a copy of the video from a mutual friend. As he would recount, years later, in a *Los Angeles Times* piece, he was knocked out by what he saw.

"The song pierced me, thrilled me and convinced me."

From that point on, it became Eustis' mission in life to sing the praises of Miranda's genius at the drop of a hat. "Lin had hit upon a subject and a form that were brilliantly suited for each other. By using the language of the streets to tell the story of our country, Lin was reclaiming a story that was meant for all people."

And it would not be long before Eustis would go straight to Miranda with his praise and make him an offer that most composers of any stripe would kill for. He invited Miranda to come work on *Hamilton* at The Public Theater. It would not be the first time the possibility of *Hamilton* going big time had been dangled in front of the young composer. With the rush of excitement from his White House appearance, Miranda had been hearing all kinds of things from all sorts of people. In those heady days, it was all-exciting and the potential for greatness seemed endless. But what most people did not take into account was that Miranda, both good and bad, was most certainly under a lot of pressure on a number of fronts.

Ever since the success of *In the Heights*, he was constantly being bombarded with the question of 'what's next?' In his gut, Miranda had seemingly already come to the conclusion that *Hamilton* was next. But *Hamilton*, at that point, was nothing more than an incomplete, fragmentary notion. He seemed enamored of the idea of *Hamilton: The Mixtape* album concept but he knew that the sheer scope of the idea was a Broadway musical in the making. Creatively, he was most likely at a crossroads. Emotionally and psychologically he was struggling. Quite simply, when it came to *Hamilton*, Miranda was just not ready.

Which was why the first time Eustis made his offer to Miranda, as he reflected in the *Los Angeles Times*, he was greeted with "It isn't a show. It's a concept album. Maybe the show will come after the album."

Eustis would not let Miranda's rebuff dissuade him. He would be patient.

Chapter Seventeen
Love and Marriage

Going into 2010, Miranda's life seemed like the proverbial busman's holiday. Although it was a given that he was spending time with his family and, in particular, Vanessa, that aspect of his life was kept low key. When it came to his creative life, what Miranda was up to was very much, and most willingly on his part, in the public eye.

Bring It On: The Musical was continuing in development at an active pace despite the fact that it was seemingly a year away from going before an audience. Miranda was also working overtime, with considerable help from his father, on what was turning into a passion project, to bring a production of *In the Heights* to Puerto Rico. And while he was shepherding the national touring company of *In the Heights* through their rehearsals the previous fall, he realized that he had not gotten the character of Usnavi out of his system. And so it would be announced that Miranda would reprise the role during the month-long run of *In the Heights* in Los Angeles, beginning June 22, 2010 at the famed Pantages Theater. "To be honest, I've been itching to play with the national cast since we began their rehearsals last fall," he reported to *Playbill.com*. "I can't wait to get back on that stage in Usnavi's shoes."

But by mid 2010, all of those plans would become less important.

Miranda could be a true romantic when he felt he had found his soulmate. Vanessa Nadal was that in spades and as the relationship quickly advanced to the level of 'serious,' he was quick to point out that the love of his life was all that and more. She was multi-degreed and multi-employed in the areas of law and science, light years from his world but intelligent in every sense of the word which only added to his attraction to her. She was comfortable, understanding and supportive in his world and would never allow him the luxury of feeling sorry for himself. If things were not going Miranda's way, creatively, he could count on Vanessa to set him straight with the notion that everybody goes through those moments and, as she offered in a tweet, "He should keep writing and get back to his piano."

During his 2008 Tony Award acceptance speech, Miranda was quick to point out Vanessa when he said, "Vanessa, who still leaves me breathless. Thank you for loving me when I was broke." On another occasion, as chronicled by *US*, he credited Vanessa for being in his corner when he experienced those dark days. "My wife's the reason anything gets done. She nudges me toward promises by degrees."

And so it was on September 5, 2010, that Miranda and Nadal would become husband and wife. But not before Miranda would offer up a full-blown theatrical extravaganza to honor his wife and their magic moment.

Sometime in early August, Miranda secretly gathered a rather non-professional group of family and friends in the New York rehearsal hall of his friend and choreographer Andy Blankenbuehler and began a month-long, stealth rehearsal. Miranda would acknowledge in a *Glamour* story that he knew he was not dealing with anything, for the most part, resembling professional performers. "What we lacked in polish, we hopefully made up for with love and joy."

The couple were married at the Belvedere Mansion in Staatsburg, New York. As Judge Rolando T. Acosta said the magic words that made Miranda and Nadal husband and wife, a chorus of Broadway singers sang majestically in the background. The ceremony was time honored, carrying with it a flourish that enhanced the joyousness of it all.

Following the conclusion of the ceremony, the wedding party and countless guests repaired to a massive tent outside on the lawn of the mansion where the celebration continued. A 22-piece orchestra provided the musical backing. The celebrity contingent was much in evidence as Ruben Blades and Gilbert Santa Rosa joined in the festivities, happily rapping along with the bride and bridegroom. The dance floor was filled to overflowing with multi generations of both families, a very cultural and ethnic vibe permeating the atmosphere. Finally, it was time for family and friends to step up to the microphone and offer best wishes to the happy couple.

First up was Nadal's father who, after a few perfunctory remarks, brought Miranda to the stage for more loving sentiments. That's when Miranda's long-planned surprise was unveiled. Miranda suddenly broke into full-throated song, uttering the now familiar refrain of *Fiddler on the Roof's* L'Chaim (To Life), complete with highly enticing dance moves. The look on Nadal's face told the tale, beaming at her now husband's theatrical dedication. The look would quickly change to one of unbridled joy when, suddenly, a literal flood of family members and friends flooded onto the stage and erupted into a full-blown song and dance extravaganza. With Miranda as the focal point, the sight of totally inexperienced relatives dancing and singing their hearts out through a fairly tight, choreographed and electric musical experience, full of spirited vocals and highly athletic, given the age of some of the participants, dance moves.

The mini-performance ended with thundering applause and cheers. Only Miranda could have pulled together such a loving and theatrical tribute to his wife. "Everyone in the performance had one thing in common," Miranda would later tell *Glamour*, "and that was that we would do anything to show how much we loved Vanessa."

Chapter Eighteen
Chasing Hamilton

Midway through 2009, author Chernow had gotten used to receiving email missives from Miranda. Questions, updates, ideas, notions about characters. Chernow knew that Miranda was serious about doing something with Hamilton. One email in particular would drive that point home as he offered in a *New York Times* conversation.

"The next thing I know, he [Miranda] sent me an email that said 'go on YouTube.' That he had just performed that first song he had played for me [now going under the title of Alexander Hamilton] at The White House and had gotten a standing ovation from the Obamas. I thought 'Wow! I am strapped to a real rocket with this young guy'."

He would discover how serious a venture he had climbed aboard over the next year. Chernow, on a seemingly regular schedule was receiving one or two songs from Miranda every month or so, each one, to the author's way of thinking, even more amazing than the next one. Miranda, by this time well ensconced in marital and domestic tranquility was, nevertheless, constantly on fire on the subject of Hamilton. While still thinking in terms of a hip hop album, the notion of

Hamilton: The Musical was becoming a real element of his creative process.

"This is Biggie, this is Tupac," he enthusiastically explained to *Playbill.com*. "This is hip hop. This is my *Jesus Christ: Superstar*, my Andrew Lloyd Webber moment. In my ideal vision for this project, we get really amazing rappers to play these different parts."

Miranda continued to remain on the fence, well into 2010, album or musical. The idea of *The Hamilton Mixtape Album* appealed to him with one telling exception, it would be an album of totally unfamiliar music with no history to it, a risky proposition both creatively and economically. To do a musical on Hamilton had its own potential pitfalls; it could easily be perceived as too stodgy for hip audiences and too ground-breakingly different for the more sedate theatergoer. It would take Vanessa and his marriage and honeymoon that same year to finally tip the scales.

"We went on our honeymoon and, again, I have the idea for Hamilton in my head," he told *Grantland.com*. "So I wrote the King George song ["You'll Be Back" which many would describe as very 60's Beatlesque] without a piano around. So we got back from our honeymoon and suddenly my producers are like '*In the Heights* is closing.' So that was the starter pistol for me. It was like 'Oh Shit! I won't have another show on Broadway which was my steady source of income.' "

Taking a cue from respected low-budget filmmaker Robert Rodriguez, Miranda decided to pull back slightly while continuing to work steadily on *Hamilton*. He continued to fine tune and basically observe the progress of *Bring It On: The Musical* which, at the time, was gearing up for a 2011 premiere run in Atlanta as a prelude to a national tour. Miranda also took the opportunity to take on his first recurring role in a network television series called *Do No Harm*.

Do No Harm, a modern retelling of *Dr. Jekyll and Mr. Hyde* set in the world of medicine, had Miranda in the recurring role of Dr. Ruben Mercado. Miranda had a good laugh in a *Grantland.com* interview as he talked about his *Do No Harm* experience. "*Do No Harm* was like a writing residency for me. It was a bad NBC show, I was sixth on the call sheet. I took the job because it shot in Philly and I was going to get killed off in the 11th episode. I wasn't interested in doing or going to Los Angeles [for pilot season] or winding up on a series and signing a seven-year contract. I would have my days free in Philly to write."

For the record, Miranda barely made it to his television death. Although receiving a commitment for 12 episodes, *Do Now Harm's* ratings were abysmal and the network cancelled the show after airing only two episodes. The remaining ten episodes would be 'burned off' in the coming months with little acknowledgement of Miranda's promised character demise in episode 11.

Needless to say, Miranda was thrilled when his character was officially pronounced dead on arrival as he excitedly tweeted shortly after he wrapped. "Last day of work on *Do No Harm*. Then I speed home to my wife and dog and get us all sick."

Miranda's approach to writing *Hamilton* took many and varied paths. Besides constantly being in contact with Chernow to critique the historical accuracy of his work, Miranda read up on every aspect of Hamilton's life and times, with particular attention paid to the books *The Heartbreak of Aaron Burr* by H.W. Brands and *Affairs of Honor* by Joanne Freeman. This seemingly more orthodox approach to creating *Hamilton: The Musical* was more than counterbalanced by his literal 'street' approach to creating the *Hamilton* soundtrack as he offered in a conversation with *Smithsonian.com*

"For *Hamilton*, what I would do is write at the piano until I had something I liked. Then I'd make a loop of it and put it in my headphones. Then I would just walk around listening to the music until I came up with the lyrics that I liked. That's where the notebooks would come in. I would sort of write what came to me, bring it back to the piano. I guess I needed to be kind of ambulatory to write lyrics."

But as he delved deeper into the Hamilton oeuvre, Miranda would find that inspiration could strike anywhere and at anytime. As was the case with the creation of the song "Wait For It'" which *Mental Floss* excerpted for its piece on unusual aspects of the creation of *Hamilton* article. "I wrote the song 'Wait For It' on the subway. I was going to a friend's house for a birthday party in Brooklyn when a lyric from the chorus of 'Wait For It' came to me. I sang the melody into my iPhone, then I went to the guy's party, stayed for 15 minutes and wrote the rest of the song on the train going back home."

Miranda's enthusiasm for *Hamilton* would go a long way toward gaining him access to historical places that would aid in the Hamilton writing process. Of particular significance was his being granted permission to use New York's Morris Jumel Mansion (the oldest existing house on Manhattan and once the temporary headquarters of George Washington during The Revolutionary War) and, in particular a bedroom once occupied by Aaron Burr as a place for him to write. Miranda found the historic vibe of Burr's room an integral element of the writing sessions that produced the songs "Wait For It" and "The Room Where It Happens'" Miranda acknowledged the irony of creating literally in the lap of history in a *New York Post* story when he said "George Washington used The Morris Jumel Mansion as a base while he was planning to flee New York. I had writing sessions and meetings for *Hamilton* there. Some writers go to The Berkshires [for Inspiration]. I went to 162nd Street."

In the meantime, *Hamilton* was not paying the bills and so, between 2010 and 2012 Miranda would take on a wide variety of acting gigs that included a guest starring role in the network sitcom *Modern Family*, a one-shot appearance in an episode of the web series *Submissions Only*, a supporting role in the movie *The Odd Life of Timothy Green*, a Coca Cola sponsored short called *The Polar Bears* and a television movie focusing on the comedy/improv antics of his side project, Freestyle Love Supreme.

Adding to the creative vortex that was Miranda's life was that *Bring It On: The Musical* was gearing up for its off Broadway and, ultimately its Broadway run through much of 2012. Miranda had done his creative due diligence on *Bring It On* with a taut musical backdrop but, ever the perfectionist, he was always on call for a quick fix or a question from the production. *Bring It On: The Musical* would ultimately have a solid, if not spectacular run, 21 preview performances and 173 shows on Broadway, before ringing down the curtain in December 2012. However the buzz of the show, not to mention Miranda's association, would immediately call for a national and international touring company to begin right around the time *Hamilton* was taking shape. Miranda was never far from busy but always was able to effectively compartmentalize so that nothing stalled.

The progress of writing the music of *Hamilton* continued at a steady, productive pace, with Miranda receiving constant feedback on the music from Chernow and, later Sondheim. Of more practical interest was the relationship between Miranda and his *In the Heights* director Thomas Kail.

Like many others in Miranda's inner circle, Kail had been alternately amused, skeptical and concerned when his young compatriot had made his initial pitch to him for *Hamilton*. As *Hamilton* had not yet morphed from a concept hip hop album to a Broadway musical, Kail kept a watchful eye and was, admittedly, impressed by the quality of the music Miranda was creating. Miranda's Tony wins and the rave notices of his Spanish language *West Side Story* and *Bring It On: The Musical* had essentially punched his ticket for him to do basically whatever he wanted. But the nagging question in hushed corners was that even if a *Hamilton* musical took place, would it ultimately fly? The theater landscape was littered with highly experimental or controversial projects that either died a critical death or a lack of interest by the public. Kail watched and waited, occasionally setting vague deadlines for Miranda getting the music together and then watching as Miranda missed the deadlines by responding with an even more expansive outpouring of music and song.

The first sign that something was about to give would come in 2011. Miranda and his group Freestyle Love Supreme had been approached to perform at the annual Ars Nova Benefit Concert. Miranda readily agreed and, at one point in the performance, took the opportunity to showcase the Hamilton song "My Shot." But, as chronicled in a compilation of tweets by *Theatermania.com*, he was still uneasy about anything connected to *Hamilton* being out in public and insisted that no cameras be allowed. "I am testing a new *Hamilton* song tonight at Ars Nova fundraiser. No cameras. The only way to hear it is to go." The song went over exceedingly well and Miranda was over the moon as he tweeted "New Hamilton song went awesome last night. This thing is gonna be my masterpiece." Kail was, likewise, sold on the fact that *Hamilton* had Broadway possibilities. During an after the show conversation with Miranda, Kail said it was time to get serious about Hamilton and he set a timeline of six months for a concert performance that would highlight all the *Hamilton* material Miranda would have written to that point.

Fate was about to give Hamilton the next leg up. The universally applauded American Songbook concert series, held annually at New York's Lincoln Center, reached out to Miranda with the opportunity to perform at the January 2012 edition. Miranda jumped at the chance, seeing it as an opportunity to test what had now become an even dozen Hamilton compositions in front of a live audience in the intimate Allen Room venue. Kail recalled in the book *Hamilton: The Revolution* that it was an opportunity for Miranda to creatively let his hair down. "We could have a band so we could orchestrate some of the songs. We could get seven or eight of our friends and just throw a party."

On the night of January 11, 2012, the 450 seat Allen Room was filled to capacity. As expected, friends and family members had come out to support Miranda and *Hamilton's* maiden voyage. Word had also gotten out along the theater community grapevine that Miranda was about to unveil what had been the much-anticipated follow up to *In the Heights* and so several members of the press as well as high level producers were also in attendance.

True to Kail's prediction, the performance had quickly become party central. The first order of business turned out to be what Miranda told the audience was "the DNA of my brain" in which he and the orchestra laid down a funky hip hop beat as they paid homage to many of Miranda's influences that included The Notorious BIG, Talib Kweli and Eminem. What followed was a sonic celebration as Miranda and company turned the evening into an electrifying preview of a full dozen songs from what would become *Hamilton: The Musical*. There was some trepidation on the young composer's part with many of the songs being performed for the first time in front of an audience that, no matter how hip, was still in the dark about what his interpretation of Hamilton would be like. What it would turn out to be was a rich, well-defined modern look at a historical figure in which words painted theatrical portraits of Hamilton and his life and times. Admittedly, many in the audience had only a rudimentary idea of who Hamilton was and how deep his story ran. But in

Miranda's hands, it all immediately came alive in a theatrical sense that was kicking open the door of theater and its inherent expectations.

By the conclusion of the performance, the audience was stunned and amazed. Among those offering up their enthusiastic congratulations was Jeffrey Seller, who produced *In the Heights*, who offered in *Hamilton: The Revolution* that he felt that, at that moment, Miranda had proven that Hamilton was on the verge of a new kind of greatness.

"It became crystal clear to everyone in the room that *Hamilton*, even at that point, was a Broadway show. I thought 'here's the show, the musical has emerged, this makes dramatic sense and it is scintillating.' Even in a concert format, the story was taking place."

Miranda was extremely upbeat at the success of The American Songbook performance when he tweeted, "Yes still writing. It's my masterpiece. And it takes time."

Chapter Nineteen
Going Public

It would turn out that Seller was not all talk and no action. Within weeks of his pronouncement that *Hamilton* had, indeed, proved road tested, the producer took separate meetings with both Miranda and Kail, outlining not only his interest but his willingness to go all in as producer and to do whatever it took to get *Hamilton* to Broadway.

Miranda's excitement at the news was palpable but it would also ignite an increased work schedule. With a dozen songs already stage worthy, *Hamilton* was barely through the first act of a perceived two-act production. How strenuous the ensuing weeks and months would be to get *Hamilton* ready for its first official unveiling was not lost on Miranda and Kail. But as author Chernow related to *Newsweek*, by the time Seller was officially on board, Miranda had long since been creating *Hamilton* a at a lightning pace.

"In the beginning we said 'we would all be dead by the time Lin finished [writing the music]' so Thomas [Kail] put him on a diet of two songs a month. And when Lin wrote the songs, he would send them to me over the internet, so I was getting the show piecemeal, one or two songs at a time. Then there came the day where he told me for the first time he was now working with actors."

And the reason Miranda was now working with actors was that the brain trust of Kail, Seller and himself had come to the conclusion that enough of *The Hamilton Mixtape's* music was in the can, 33 songs to that point, to consider *The Hamilton Mixtape* was ready for a real public airing. Enter the prestigious Powerhouse Theater Reading Festival, presented annually by Vassar College, which showcased promising shows in their embryonic stage via intimate readings.

It was agreed that Miranda, Kail and Lacamoire would convene at the Vassar campus for an eight-day cram course prior to putting *Hamilton* before the public. Miranda had arrived first, followed by Kail who knocked on the door and was immediately taken aback by what he saw. "He [Miranda] answered the door and was all bandaged up," he remembered in *Playbill.com*. "He was like 'I brought my skateboard and I rode it down the hall.' The dude was on a skateboard and just seeing him standing there was a moment of like 'I must have broken all the rules but I'm okay.'"

Lacamoire soon joined them and, as it turned out, living together in one room, constantly bouncing ideas off each other at breakfast or chasing after Miranda on another skateboard adventure, was quite productive. Kail related that being in an isolated place away from the big city and the business side of what they were attempting to do, got their creative juices flowing. "I knew that we could go there and create whatever environment we needed to suit what the show was requiring at the moment."

The early version, out of necessity, had evolved

at a lightning pace which, in turn, meant Miranda was suddenly faced with needing some semblance of a cast for the Vassar reading.

"Well it's in *The New York Times*," Miranda tweeted. "My Hamilton deadline is real now."

His sense of ethnic pride and belief in diversity which had served Miranda so well in *In the Heights* was very much in evidence in choosing the cast for the Vassar performances. Above all, they had to be talented. In some cases, he was familiar with their work from *In the Heights*. Multi-racial was not far behind as Miranda, most likely on a subconscious level at that point, was flying in the face of any preconceived notion that a musical about Hamilton had to be staffed by a primarily white cast. In any event, the final cast list for the very first incarnation of *The Hamilton Mixtape* would consist of Miranda, Javier Munoz, Utkarsh Ambudkar, Ana Nogueira, Anika Noni Rose, David Deeds, Joshua Henry, Presilah Nunez, Christopher Jackson and Isaiah Johnson.

Miranda was excited at the prospect of having real actors aboard and excitedly tweeted the thrill of the first time his cast gathered for a table reading. "We got some actors around a table, singing new *Hamilton* today because my demos [at this point] are nigh unlistenable."

The Vassar performances would provide particular challenges for Miranda. Although there had been some speculation that the arc of *The Hamilton Mixtapes* might resort to an actual script that would include dialogue and characterization between the musical numbers, that element of Hamilton was far from being set in stone.

But while Miranda would not completely dismiss

that notion, he felt what he was doing was way too personal to consider an outside element. The reading would consist of the singers performing that early stage of the musical through song, rap and spoken word elements. *The Hamilton Mixtapes* would open and close on July 27, 2014. Tickets for what was slotted as two afternoon performances were gobbled up immediately and a waiting list for last minute cancellations was just as quickly filled to capacity.

The Vassar readings would consist of Act One and 30 songs and a handful of three songs from the still largely in progress Act Two. The response was overwhelmingly enthusiastic and positive and indicated to Miranda that he was, most certainly, onto something. Miranda managed to keep his acting chops up during this period on a couple of low profile jobs, narrating duties on an episode of the popular public radio show *This American Life* (This American Life: One Night Only At BAM) for which he wrote much of his appearances' music including a comedy mini musical entitled *21 Chump Street*, and a small part in an original web series called *Studio Heads.*

But by late 2014, everything but *Hamilton* had become merely a brief dalliance or a way to turn a buck. Miranda's obsession was Hamilton had reached emotional critical mass and as he would tell both *CNBC* and *Rolling Stone*, it was often overwhelming to the point of madness. "I was in love with this idea. Hamilton would not leave me alone. When I was walking the dog, when I was taking a shower. He was like 'write me.' It would take me six years to write that fucking show. You can only do that if you are in love with your subject."

Miranda's obsession with Hamilton was only matched by the lengths he would often go with tracking down the minute in history that would inspire or give him new insight into the Hamilton mystique. During regular breaks from *Hamilton's* development, Miranda, occasionally with director Kail, would scour the East Coast, looking for historical landmarks related to Hamilton in particular and the Revolutionary War in general. Miranda was very much the tourist on those occasions, visibly enthralled as he marveled at the sheer significance of such as Hamilton Grange, Valley Forge and the Fraunces Tavern where George Washington gave a heartfelt speech to his officers on the occasion of defeating the British in a pivotal Revolutionary War battle.

"I met the director of The Museum of American Finance and he showed me a plaque on the side of an office building that said this was Thomas Jefferson's residence in New York," he offered to *The New Yorker*. "I love that we are just a bunch of layers where all this shit went down."

It has never been made clear whether Miranda's excursions actually helped Miranda in creating the musical platform for *Hamilton* but it was a certainty that being in the presence of history must have easily set the table. One particular excursion to New Jersey and the spot of the infamous Hamilton/Burr duel took place, would ultimately leave Miranda caught in a time warp of the past and the present and how society tends to treat its historical past. The very spot where Hamilton would be killed was now locked behind a locked gate, down a slope and surrounded by apartment complexes. "I didn't expect the site to be that manicured," he told *The New Yorker*. "I thought there would be some woods to walk around in."

The upswing in interest generated by the Vassar reading of *Hamilton* had the desired effect of generating some financial interest, to the tune of $175,000 in development money to help advance Miranda's brainchild up the ladder to a full blown production.

But for Miranda, *Hamilton* was not an easy sell, even to those already championing the production. Miranda knew going in that he was bucking a tradition bound and psychologically entrenched system. And when it came to how to proceed, even Miranda would have his doubts. Still lingering was the notion that Hamilton as a production would be sung, especially in hip hop rap stylings that might be alien to many in the audience and might need a seasoned playwright's touch to keep the show on track. Miranda was skeptical but more than willing to give a counter balance to the music a chance.

"We actually went down the road with a playwright at one point," he told *Grantland.com*. "There's a very early version of Act One where we had songs and they were the songs that were in the show. But we found that if you start with an opening number you can't go back to a speech because the ball is just thrown too high in the air."

Then there was the question of casting *Hamilton*. Miranda was insistent that Hamilton would be colorblind and, as he had shown in The American Songbook and Vassar performances, he was not above casting all ethnicities even in what were traditionally perceived as roles for white actors. Casting decisions were made easier to digest, largely due to the hip hop musical nature of what Miranda had created. Which in itself brought up the question of whether a musical driven totally by hip hop and rap would prove mind numbing to the typical theatergoer, far removed from the idea or universe of street music.

But Miranda stood his ground and even those with reservations could not doubt his enthusiasm and drive to make *Hamilton* his way, a reflection of the world as it was funneled through a world as it was today.

Miranda's reluctance to commit to a full-blown Hamilton musical was, by 2014, beginning to crack. The success of The American Songbook and Vassar presentations had encouraged him, as had the continued high quality of the music he was creating for this still unspecified project. Eustis would continue to, good naturedly, tempt Miranda, as would close members of his creative team, specifically Kail and Seller. Kail acknowledged as much in a *Washington Post* interview when, after harkening back to the impact of the White House performance, offered, "We sensed something was happening here that could live beyond a concert album, as a show. There was a story to tell.' Seller, in the same article, was equally excited about *Hamilton's* potential. "I believe that this [*Hamilton*] is affirming in the most visceral way our pride in our country. In a way that has never happened in our lifetime."

Miranda was in deep thought about the future of *Hamilton* well into 2014. A decision was finally made in early March when it was announced that *Hamilton: The Musical* would be part of The Public Theater's

119

2014-2015 season. March 2014 would also be notable in Miranda's world when Vanessa announced that she was pregnant.

Miranda could barely stifle a laugh some years later when he told a *Los Angeles Times* reporter how he got the news that he was about to become a father. "My wife was going on a business trip and she was leaving first thing in the morning. She turned to me and said, 'You're gonna be a father. I gotta go catch a plane. And I went 'What? That's great!' And I fell back asleep."

Chapter Twenty
How to Make a *Moana*

But he did not stay asleep long.

Shortly after a call to Vanessa confirmed that, yes, she was pregnant and that, yes, he was going to be a father, Miranda received an unexpected phone call from the Disney Studios' directors John Musker and Ron Clements with an offer he most certainly could not refuse, especially since he would soon have another mouth to feed. The job struck at Miranda's love of all things Disney, being a part of a three-way writing team that would create the music for an animated feature that was still in its infancy and would not hit the screens until 2016.

Moana.

Moana tells an almost vintage Disney tale about a young Pacific Island girl who grows up while on an adventure to save her family and community. As laid out by the filmmakers, *Moana* would be backed by wall-to-wall songs, done up in a traditional Pacific Island/ calypso style. Miranda had often proclaimed his love for Disney animated films as pivotal moments in his childhood, a favorite being *The Little Mermaid* which, coincidentally, offered up similar musical stylings to what was being planned with *Moana*. It was that knowledge, coupled with Miranda's ability to tell stories with lyrics, that made Miranda a seemingly ideal choice and, in a *Los Angeles Times* conversation, Musker also allowed that timing also had a lot to do with it.

"In our astute minds, we thought *Hamilton* might come and go with no accolades. We were happy we met Lin before he was engulfed in the *Hamilton* tsunami."

Miranda would later explain to *The Hollywood Reporter* that the phone call and the offer came at an ideal time for him. Although preparation for *Hamilton* was still in its early stages, he was feeling a sense of tension and restlessness about the project and was ready for something to at least, temporarily, take his mind off *Hamilton*.

"There's an adage that if you want something done, ask a busy person to do it because they are already in motion. *Moana* provided an oasis in the general hecticness of my life in the *Hamilton* era and it goes without saying that I thrive under a deadline."

It also did not hurt that Miranda would be working with two other film music composers, veteran Disney musicsmith Mark Mancina and Samoan musician and composer Opetaia Foa'i. To Miranda's way of thinking, working with others while as opposed to creating music primarily on his own as he had been doing had its appeal. "This felt heaven sent for me," he told *Variety*. "The fun for me working in theater has always been about collaboration and the idea that the best idea in the room wins."

Literally days after that initial call, Miranda and Mancina were on a plane heading for New Zealand and a get to know you meeting between them and Foa'i which consisted of the trio attending a music festival that featured a lot of South Pacific music. Then it was off to a studio in a remote countryside where the trio would spend a number of days getting to know each other, listening to music and jamming together. The three composers would emerge from the studio creatively and personality wise aligned and ready to tackle what would be two plus years of creating the music of *Moana*.

Admittedly, Miranda was not wise to the way Disney did business and so he was somewhat amused when, upon returning to the states, he was asked to sign a bunch of papers essentially telling him that he could not talk to anyone about what he was doing in regards to *Moana*. In an interview with *Vulture.com*, Miranda had a good laugh at all the secrecy, although he did understand the reasoning behind it all. "I do have a reputation for being a bit of an over sharer on Twitter. So I signed a nondisclosure agreement when I started writing these songs. Only my family and a couple of close friends knew what I was doing."

On the surface, balancing his day-to-day life surrounding *Hamilton* with his moonlighting on *Moana* over what would ultimately take in the next two plus years of his life seemed a herculean task. But it would be one that Miranda, who had always had a knack for compartmentalizing, would figure out. On the upside, the progress of *Hamilton* in the theatrical world had given Miranda even more notoriety which meant more press, more elevator pitches. Miranda was realistic in dealing with the consequences of being 'the next big thing' as he offered in the *Los Angeles Times*. "In one sense it was really great because when something is as successful as *Hamilton* was becoming, everyone wants a piece of you."

By the time *Hamilton* was making its way to Off Broadway, Miranda figured out that the best way to fit *Moana* into his life was to begin saying no to a lot of things. "I had to really protect my writing time," he told the *Los Angeles Times*. "Tuesdays and Thursdays were full -time *Moana* writing days. I would meet via Skype with the creative writing team at 5:00 p.m. every Tuesday and Thursday. Then I would go to the chiropractor. Then I would get into costume for a 7:00 p.m. show. Time for *Moana* was built into my performance schedule."

Going in, *Moana* was a blank slate when it came to the music. But with Miranda and his writing partners immediately in sync, the process immediately took on an organic tone and, as Miranda told *The Hollywood Reporter*, a symbiotic shorthand. "If I would play a rhythm and Opetaia would make a face, I knew that was not a rhythm that would not come from his part of the world and I would throw it out and start from scratch.'

Two songs that encapsulate how well this three way writing job worked were "We Know the Way" and "How Far I'll Go." Miranda acknowledged in *The Hollywood Reporter* that, "We Know The Way" pretty much set the tone for all the songs in terms of the working relationship. "It worked so organically that 'We Know The Way' set the template for the rest of our collaboration. Opetaia gave us the melody and a sense of the words as they would have been said by the tribe's ancestors. I was just doing my best to translate the words of the ancestors in a way that would fit Opetaia's melody. Then Mark started playing guitar and the chords on the second chorus. That song best represents creating something bigger than the some of its parts."

Which Miranda recalled put him in good stead over the life of this three-cornered creative process. "I wouldn't bring in a finished song. I'd bring in a verse or a chorus and go 'Am I headed in the right direction?' "

But the collaboration did not begin and end with merely creating the songs. *Moana* was shaping up as a big film for Disney. There was a lot of excitement surrounding the film and, as such, translated into a lot of suggestions from a lot of different quarters. Over the life of writing *Moana*, Miranda and his collaborators were subject to copious 'notes' from studio executives, the directors, screenwriters and, on occasion, filmmakers who had nothing to do with *Moana* but had experience on other Disney animated films.

Miranda recalled constantly hearing about how a certain song was making a portion of the film drag or that some elements of the music might be better suited for another section of the film. What it often translated into was that Miranda and his collaborators were sent back to already completed material for a redo. Miranda recalled to *Vulture.com* that patience was always a virtue in the aftermath of receiving questions that ultimately led to suggestions. "You would end up going back to the drawing board over and over again with an eye toward clarifying the journey."

The release of *Moana* and the Broadway run of *Hamilton* were pretty much a dead heat in 2016. Miranda would often admit to being creatively exhausted by the end of his time with *Moana* but was finally satisfied with the idea of working on a Disney movie and the challenges that the experience allowed him to overcome. "Writing is lonely work," he told *The Hollywood Reporter*. "For me, the most fun was getting to bring something into a room with a bunch of other artists and saying 'Let's kick the tires on it and make it better.'"

Chapter Twenty-One
Many Miles to Go

One could pretty much set their clock by Miranda during 2014. And the only thing that was certain was that he was running fast. At home at every opportunity, Miranda was very much the doting father-to-be, attentive to Vanessa's every need, regardless of day, time or circumstance. Away from his husbandly duties, Miranda remained very much the breadwinner, working literally night and day on *Hamilton* while taking on occasional side projects to test his creativity as well as to bring in some extra money...

...Which included a guest-starring role in the Bedtime Stories episode of the television series *How I Met Your Mother*. Miranda would also make a handful of appearances as part of the comedy rock duo *The Skivvies* whose live show consisted of performing musical mash-ups in their underwear. He would also take his acting chops back to the theater with an appearance in the revival of *Tick Tick Boom* as part of the Encores! Off Center series of plays. And with the nearly non-existent free time, he managed to write the music for a new tune for the new season of *Sesame Street*.

But through it all, *Hamilton* and the many machinations of mounting a Broadway quality play remained uppermost in Miranda's mind. Even Miranda had to admit that he could not do it all himself and so he was quick to bring in his brain trust from *In the Heights*, besides Kail as de facto director, Andy Blankenbuehler and Alex Lacamoire were once again on board as choreographer and musical orchestration respectively. Seller would remain a solid and subtle addition, guiding Miranda through the business and reality of mounting the show. His suggestions to Miranda, even on a minute level, struck at the practical side of show business. A case in point being that, while Miranda insisted on calling his creation *The Hamilton Mixtape* well into the development of the show, Seller, through gentle but constant nudging, finally convinced Miranda to shorten the title to *Hamilton*.

When not continuing work on the musical elements of *Hamilton* which, in typical Miranda fashion was growing well beyond expectations and would, most certainly, require some whittling down at some point, Miranda would often be found monitoring a seemingly endless round of auditions as every actor on the East Coast and beyond scrambled for a shot at what was shaping up as the role of a lifetime for anybody lucky enough to make the cut.

It was a given that Miranda would once again take on the role of Hamilton but beyond that it was anybody's guess. He had developed quite a few friendships during the American Songbook and Vassar days and, in a perfect world, would like to take some of those actors along for the Broadway ride. But at the end of the day, talent would ultimately win out over loyalty and friendship.

Midway through 2014, the cast for *Hamilton* was

announced. Those making the transition from the workshop group to the Off Broadway cast were Miranda, Daveed Diggs and Christopher Jackson. Newcomers included Phillipa Soo, Leslie Odom Jr., Renee Elise Goldsberry, Brian D'Arcy James, Anthony Ramos, Jasmine Cephas Jones and Okieriete Onaodowan.

Miranda was thrilled at the choices, feeling that the actors had a real affinity for his creation. But there was little time to rejoice. 2014 was almost over and there was still much for Miranda to do. And with so much to do and Miranda's often lax attitude toward making deadlines, he often found himself literally composing *Hamilton* on the fly or, as he offered in a tongue in cheek tweet collected by *Theater Mania.com*, or on the bus.

"Finishing a tune at 10:30 for actors who are learning it at 11. When will I stop doing my homework on the bus?"

But as the weeks and months wound down, there seemed to be reminders at every turn that *Hamilton's* development had reached critical mass. There were days when Miranda would marvel as Lacamoire would patiently teach the cast and orchestra how to handle bits of music that Miranda had just handed it hours earlier. There were also the seemingly endless meetings of the *Hamilton* 'cabinet' that went long into the next and early morning in which Miranda, Kail, Lacamoire and Blankenbuehler sat hunched over computers, listening to countless playbacks of the songs and trying to decide which cast member should sing a particular song.

By late October, there was also the matter of

having too much music to comfortably fit into the two-act. Miranda, in a blog, had a good laugh at the fact that, as it was coming down to crunch time, he had written too much. "There are 52 songs in *Hamilton* right now. I think I can get it down to a lean 48."

In the later months of 2014, the inner workings of *Hamilton*'s development seemed in a constant state of flux. A first act that had seemed set in stone from the beginning was suddenly being questioned as what kind of climactic moment would prime the pump, historically, for Act Two. An endless number of workshops were presented in an attempt to refine and develop all of the show's integral elements. When he was not tweaking and turning every conceivable element of the production's music, Miranda was hard at work on the *Hamilton* book.

And then there was the specter of impending fatherhood constantly at Miranda's back. Vanessa's pregnancy, by all reports, had been stress-free and, speculation was, that Miranda preoccupation with *Hamilton* had probably made the pregnancy less so. But no one in Miranda's inner circle could doubt that the composer was always on call and alert when it came to the needs of his wife.

November was turning into crunch time for *Hamilton*. With the show scheduled to open Off Broadway in less than two months, *Hamilton: The Musical* (as it was still informally being called at that point) seemed primed and ready, minus of course the endless final round of corrections, questions and changes, typical of most theatrical productions, but particularly intense when, at Miranda's insistence, that both the historical integrity of the characters and the times and how it all played off the hip hop elements of the show.

Miranda was in a manic state, buzzing from one element of the production to another, often appearing exhausted but always seeming to mask it with that perpetual boy-like grin. Miranda could sense that something wondrous was about to happen.

And then it did. Vanessa went into labor.

On November 10, 2014, Miranda tweeted the following, "The screams reach a frenzied pitch. Sebastian Miranda enters. He is 7 pounds, 10 ounces. End of Act 1."

Chapter Twenty-Two
The Power Play

Miranda was well aware of the power he was beginning to wield. He most certainly felt the adulation and 'next big thing' status that had arisen in the wake of his *In the Heights* triumph. And he had seen signs that real celebrity was on the horizon. He was being spotted and acknowledged on the street. Miranda would willingly pose for selfies and sign autographs. Owing to his growing reputation in the theater community, upfront money and offers to perform his works in prestigious venues had become part of his world. Name peers wanted to get to know him. But Miranda was still a babe in the woods when it came to the trappings of his growing notoriety. It was all fun and games when compared to what was really driving him. But anyone who broached the subject during those heady days in 2014 certainly had a sense that he was aware of the growing sense of celebrity that was beginning to envelop him.

In conversation with *Fast Company.com*, it was obvious that he was maintaining his ego and was philosophical about the fact that he was on the cusp of something big in the public's eye. "I mean it's insane," he reflected. "All eyes are on me and the world is calling. I am aware that there is a giant spotlight on me."

By July 20 2014, the spotlight was shining particularly bright. That was the day tickets for the Off Broadway run of *Hamilton* went on sale. Whether they wanted to admit it or not, Miranda and his inner circle would hold their collective breath. Early ticket sales did not necessarily dictate a show's future but lackluster early sales could easily sink a production like *Hamilton* in the public eye months before it was set to open. Because in pop culture and, in particular, the world of theater, perception was everything. Fortunately, first sales were extremely positive but, despite the good sale, *Hamilton* was still being considered in many quarters a dicey proposition.

This early feedback only seemed to add additional pressure to Miranda who, by year's end, was already burning the candle at too many ends. At the final series of rehearsals, Miranda was conspicuous by the fatigue on his face. With a newborn in the house, it was a given that neither Miranda nor Vanessa were getting much sleep. Throw in the seemingly round the clock preparations, additions and subtractions and everything last minute, all geared toward *Hamilton*'s January start of live shows and it was little wonder that Miranda was often seemingly in a daze as he recalled his feelings in the days leading up the *Hamilton's* Off Broadway debut.

"At opening night at The Public Theater, I remember thinking 'soon everything will go back to normal.' And that just never happened."

As the days drew closer, Miranda and company were left to deal with all manner of minutia in connection to the show. After literally a year of contemplation in which Miranda went back and forth on whether he would play the role of Hamilton or Aaron Burr (although he had, in fact, been playing Hamilton since the show's creative inception). He finally came down firmly on Hamilton, the feeling being that the role would play to Miranda's dramatic/flamboyant strengths. And then it came down to that old devil marketing and just what to call *Hamilton*. The producers were concerned that labeling *Hamilton* a 'Hip Hop Musical' would, somehow, limit the audience to what Miranda and others hoped would be a multi-generational crowd. The debate on that one lingered a while before perception was finally just cast to the winds. *Hamilton* was what it was meant to be and labeling be damned.

It was all butterflies and nervous excitement on the night of January 20, 2015. Not surprisingly, Miranda, all smiles and animated, could not stand still, reportedly pacing in tight circles and, by degrees, lost in thought. His second child was about to be born.

Three hours later and the buzz that had been carrying on around *Hamilton* was justified. The musical, even in its Off Broadway incarnation, was near perfect, a raw, visceral celebration of the power of theater to both entertain and educate. Miranda, as Hamilton, was a dynamo of motion and emotion as he prowled the stage telling and narrating through song, the fact and emotion of the character and the times. Cold hard historical facts immediately took on a vibrant new life when wrapped in the arms of hip hop, rap and no small amount of soul. One show in and *Hamilton* had mesmerized an audience in a way they most certainly had not been captivated in years.

And as those first few preview shows played out, critics were standing in line to heap praise on Miranda's creation. *The New York Times* proclaimed, "*Hamilton* persuasively transfers a thoroughly archived past into an unconditional present tense. It exudes the dizzying urgency of being caught up in momentous events as they occur." *The Hollywood Reporter* chimed in "There's rarely been a history lesson as entertaining as Lin-Manuel Miranda's hip hop infused musical. Miranda's work is remarkably faithful to the historical facts, imparting great amounts of information in rollicking fashion." *The New York Post* reported, "At it's best, *Hamilton* is giddily exciting. Miranda's lyrics burst with smart internal rhythms and wordplay."

And as simple as that, *Hamilton* became something more, a literal force of nature that had taken the theater world by storm. The Public Theater and its 300 seats became historical ground zero for something larger than just about anything one could imagine that had ever taken place in the history of live theater. And from that first performance, *Hamilton* was like a runaway train in the best possible way. The entire run of *Hamilton* at The Public Theater was an immediate sell out. There would be no rush lines for last minute tickets because, through what would be the entire Off Broadway run, there were none.

What there would be for Miranda during the Off Broadway run of *Hamilton* would be a bit of self-discovery. There was the real world, fatherhood, attention to family and trying to live day to day as normally as possible. In that world Miranda could still walk down the street like a regular guy. But he knew it

135

was getting harder. The counter was that each night, for a little under three hours, he was living the fantasy as the fiery Hamilton who, as Miranda was want to reveal, that the fantasy of Hamilton was allowing him to escape for a while and be all the creative things his soul wanted to be.

He was also finding that the relative intimacy of The Public Theater was proving instrumental in keeping a fairly tight and, yes normal, lid on the sense of Miranda as superstar. "When we did the show Off Broadway, there was no barrier between the cast and the audience," he offered to *GQ*. "We would just go into the lobby of The Public Theater (after a performance) and everyone was there and it was just so civil. The crowd's were smaller because there were only 300 people at a time and we just talked to everyone. No one was pushy and there was no tense energy."

The Off Broadway run of *Hamilton* was far from a finished product. Over the course of those pre-Broadway shows, the production would reportedly eliminate approximately a dozen songs and the structure of the entire show would be manipulated to form a more streamlined whole. Consequently, while putting up with the rigors of being onstage every night in the title role, behind the scenes Miranda was constantly having to fine tune *Hamilton* into what many were already predicting would be on its way to Broadway in a matter of months.

Public Theater's Eustis fondly remembered in an *American Theater* piece how nimble Miranda could be when changes were necessary. "There was a rewrite that he did on a song called "Washington on Your

Side." It was funny, dark and fully expressed but it didn't move the action of the play forward. So Lin activated the song by making it the song in which Jefferson resigns from the cabinet. It's just beautiful to watch him figure out how to make a beautiful thing and then activate it so it unleashes its full dramatic potential. That's the kind of brain he has."

Into February 2015, Hamilton had literally taken on a life of its own. Now a certified cultural phenomena, the show and its creator were on everybody's lips, *Hamilton* was on billboards, magazine covers and in hundreds of newspaper articles. Many saw the production of that once in a lifetime commercial success. Miranda saw it as the vindication of a long shot idea, incorporating his core spiritual, emotional and creative values, that had struck home with a generation ripe for a change and that were willing to follow Miranda and *Hamilton* along for the ride.

Bottom line, *Hamilton* continued to do sell out business with no end in sight. Which suddenly put Miranda and his creative team on the horns of a dilemma. It was nearing the end of the announced Off Broadway run and already there was serious talk about *Hamilton* making its Broadway debut at the Richard Rodgers Theater sometime in mid 2015 and just in time for the predicted boatload of Tony nominations. But Miranda was never far from taking his audience into consideration, and the fact that once *Hamilton* hit Broadway many would be priced out of affording tickets, acknowledged as much when he agreed to extend the Off Broadway run to April 5 and, sometime later, to May 3.

Hamilton's Off Broadway run was extended but

by February 25, it's Broadway future was already set in stone. The cast would largely remain from the Off Broadway production. But the decision to open up in August 2015 would effectively keep *Hamilton* out of Tony consideration for that year. There had been talk of rushing the production out in the spring in order to qualify but, collectively, the *Hamilton* brain trust felt there was still too much work to be done to risk a flawed Broadway debut. That scheduling setback aside, *Hamilton* continued to be a juggernaut well into May when it was announced that there would be no further extensions of the Off Broadway run and that the next stop for *Hamilton* would be Broadway.

With the transition now set in place, Miranda now seemingly had a semblance of free time. Which gave him more family time and the opportunity to indulge an unexpected opportunity which was typical of the spontaneity that marked Miranda's world.

Director J.J. Abrams, according to anecdotes delivered on *The Tonight Show*, was in the process of completing *Star Wars: The Force Awakens* when he took a day off to take in a *Hamilton* matinee. After the show, he was introduced to Miranda and the two began talking about *Star Wars*. At one point, Miranda jokingly offered his services in writing a *Star Wars* touchstone, the background music for the cantina scene. When perennial *Star Wars* composer John Williams declined to do that particular piece, the joke suddenly became reality when Abrams emailed Miranda with the missive "I know you were kidding but if you actually want to write that music." Miranda's response was equally succinct "I'll drop everything." For the next two months, Miranda worked on the music in between shows and other *Hamilton*-related business, exchanging musical files with Abrams and hammering out an ambitious piece of music in which he sang, played instruments and wrote lyrics for what would become the track "Jabba's Flow," written in the language of *Star Wars* character Jabba the Hut.

Midway through 2015, *Hamilton* was also beginning to make its presence felt during awards season, racking up numerous nominations and wins from the likes of The Lucille Lortell Awards, The Outer City Circle Awards and The Drama League Awards. Typical of the team oriented nature of the production, the music, choreography and direction were among those winning top honors. But what had to be particularly warming was the individual awards Miranda received for Outstanding Musical, Outstanding Lead Actor in a Musical and Outstanding New Score. Not too surprisingly was that Miranda's response to the accolades was low key. "I'm incredibly humbled," he told *CNBC*. "It was really overwhelming to see how this part of US history had been awakened within a younger generation."

Hamilton was scheduled to begin its Broadway previews on July 13, leading to an August 6 official Broadway debut. There was much preparation that mimicked the development of the Off Broadway run, the casting (although most of the Off Broadway cast went to the Broadway production), last minute pruning of and additions to the existing storylines.

But through it all, Miranda would manage some quiet moments, wandering the streets where he grew up and where he now lived with his own family. On one such day, Miranda and his father, Luis, were caught in a rare moment, waxing nostalgic and playful in a conversation only a father and son could have. A conversation that eventually found its way to the present and to a degree to the future. Luis was wistful as he talked, in front of a *Playbill* interviewer, about what his son's success meant. "I know that it would all be fantastic. I didn't realize that it would change his life."

Miranda smiled at his father's pronouncement. "And we're still figuring out how that was going to happen."

Chapter Twenty-Three
Lights Are Bright

Nobody would blame Miranda if he developed a swelled head behind the success of *Hamilton*.

As far back as the pre-Off Broadway days, he was already being crowned a genius, a wunderkind and just about any accolade one could imagine. Even those who knew the real Miranda were quick to dub him "a modern day Shakespeare." But as *Hamilton* moved toward its July 13, 2015 premiere at The Richard Rodgers Theater, Miranda was doing his level best to keep his head on straight. And his father was not surprised, seeing in his son the same thing he always knew he possessed. "What I admire most about him is his humility," his father Luis told *NEA.com*

He was quick to acknowledge that having his first child during the Off Broadway run and the sheer stamina it took to carry off nearly three hours a performance on a nightly basis went a long way toward keeping him grounded. But when pressed, one could sense ego mixed with pride of accomplishment in dissecting just what *Hamilton* had become.

"I don't know how many really good ideas you get in a lifetime," he told *Billboard,* "but telling *Hamilton* as a hip hop story was definitely one. It is a

141

hit show so your life changes. But I'm trying not to let it change me too much."

In hindsight, *Hamilton's* march to Broadway had seemed pre-ordained. From its first performance, the show had connected on an almost familial way with its audience and, in particular, a young, multi-generational demographic. People were fanatic in spreading the word on how wonderful the *Hamilton* experience had been and were often moving heaven and earth to find a ticket to see it again. It was a sense of loyalty that had its roots in the way Miranda and his compatriots had chosen to do business. For the actors, it had been a generous performing contract that had included a rarely seen percentage of royalties. Which was why, when it came time to take the next big step, all but one of the Off Broadway cast, happily made the transition to Broadway.

There was also the sense among everybody connected with the production that this was a once in a lifetime opportunity to be part of something that would truly last through the ages. There were a myriad of reasons why *Hamilton* was successful and there was no reason to think its Broadway run would be any different.

While on a two month hiatus between the conclusion of the Off Broadway run and the beginning of the Broadway shows, Miranda was often seen in his old Inwood neighborhood, making time for family and friends and, occasionally spotted walking his dog and making a couple of club appearances with Freestyle Love Supreme. But Miranda's thoughts were never far from *Hamilton's* Broadway debut and the need to streamline the production which resulted in a polish that would trim 15 minutes of the performances' running time. "If it's good, why not make it better," quipped Miranda in a *Smithsonian.com* piece.

By July 12, one day before the very first Off Broadway performance. *The New York Times* reported that over 200,000 tickets had been sold for the run of *Hamilton*. Even before its first Off Broadway show, *Hamilton* had officially been proclaimed the theatrical event of the year. Which translated into high ticket prices, an at times out of control secondary ticket market and, finally, the inability of many people who should be seeing *Hamilton* to afford a ticket. It was that latter issue that hit Miranda hard and so, with the aid of his producers, he inaugurated what was called the Ham4Ham pre-show lottery in which front row and some standing room only seats (reportedly about 20 seats per performance) were sold two hours before show time for $10 (the denomination of US currency in which Hamilton's face appears). The lottery commenced on July 13 when a crowd estimated at 700 people showed up outside The Richard Rodgers Theatre for a chance at the cheap seats.

The lottery was an immediate success. But it also left a lot of people disappointed. Miranda, in a *The Junto.com* story, attempted to assuage the feelings of those who did not get a ticket when he stated, "We're probably going to be here for a while. So don't be disappointed if you don't win today."

Opening night. July 13. Literally days before the first Broadway show, *Hamilton* was officially in the black. But as Miranda and the rest of the company readied themselves backstage, there was a palpable sense of excitement and nervous energy in the air.

Being a financial success was one thing. Now all Miranda and his cast had to do was go out on stage and make good on the promise.

The opening night was, most certainly, an immediate reintroduction and reimagining of *Hamilton* at its most audacious and enlightening. Streamlining the production did little to negate the sheer power, majesty and excitement that reinforced the notion of hip hop and history as a very real and legitimate art form and the newly minted gatekeeper of the coming progressive theater. Miranda in the lead role was never less than dynamic, alternately flamboyant and looking inward, he, as well as the by now seasoned cast, gloomed onto the excitement of opening night as a springboard to something even better.

And the reviewers in the audience were quick to pick up on the vibe of *Hamilton 2.0*.

The New York Times reported "I am loath to tell people to mortgage their houses and lease their children to acquire tickets to a hit Broadway show but *Hamilton* might just be worth it." *Time Out New York* enthused "I love *Hamilton*! I love it like Broadway when it gets it right. And this is so right!" *The Boston Globe's* critique was equally effusive "In his stylish and electrifying *Hamilton*, Miranda fuses the immediacy and storytelling power of hip hop and R&B with the revolutionary passions of a new nation heaving itself into existence."

Not surprisingly, celebrities across all strata of society were being drawn to *Hamilton*. People as diverse as Ron Chernow, Busta Rhymes, Stephen Sondheim and Andrew Lloyd Webber caught early performances of *Hamilton*. And Miranda was like a kid in a candy store as he would name drop and recall seeing them in the audience watching his show and his performance. "It's amazing when your heroes come to see your show," he gushed to *American Theater*. "There's always going to be a kick about that."

But even Miranda's pride at being observed by the famous had to pale shortly before opening night when he was told that President Barack Obama requested tickets for himself, his daughter, his sister and her husband for the sixth preview performance, an afternoon matinee. *Hamilton* had long held a fascination for politicians. During the Off Broadway run, no lesser lights than Bill and Hillary Clinton and Dick Cheney had witnessed his show up close and personal. But the idea of a sitting President of The United States requesting tickets...Well for Miranda that was the ultimate.

"It was the day before our very first preview," he reminisced with *Billboard*, "and we were told that he was coming to the Saturday matinee. But I don't do the Saturday matinee. That's when my alternate goes on and that was my first chance to see the show. So there was a moment of 'Do you want to go on? It's the President.' But it actually gave us an opportunity to send the message to the world that the show is the star of the show and it doesn't matter if I'm on or not. And besides, I had already had the good fortune to perform for the President."

For Miranda, having the current President in the audience for his version of *Hamilton* that was dealing with history and issues in a decidedly modern musical setting was the ultimate synchronicity.

"It was a surreal experience," Miranda told *The*

New York Times. "It was a kick to see the first three Presidents of the United States on stage while I was sitting with our current President."

There is not much that can phase New Yorkers but the sight of a Presidential motorcade moving up West 46th Street to a stop outside The Richard Rodgers Theater while members of the President's security team were seemingly everywhere, did indeed cause heads to turn. Audience members filing through the lobby for that performance had an idea something was up when the security was extra tight. But it did not take long for word to filter through the theater that the afternoon's performance would have a very special guest.

Consequently, when Obama and his family were ushered to their seats, the excitement had already reached a fever pitch and, despite warnings for security reasons, people began approaching the President and snapping selfies. Owing to a chance schedule, Miranda would not be performing in that performance but his absence from the stage was more than balanced, for Miranda, by the opportunity to sit near the President as he saw the complete production for the first time.

"He was two rows behind me," Miranda told *Billboard,* "so I kind of could not do it [see the President's reaction]. But my director Tommy Kail said he was super attentive and soaking it in and, at one point during the King George number, Obama actually started slapping his leg."

According to reports filed by several local publications including *The New York Times*, Obama sat intently as he watched the performance, occasionally bobbing his head in time to the music. During intermission, the President went backstage and chatted and took photographs with the *Hamilton* cast who were, reportedly, beside themselves with excitement.

With the conclusion of the performance, the President and his entourage were whisked away amid a phalanx of secret service officers. Miranda, post performance and quoted by *The New York Times*, was in awe of what having the President see his creation meant to him. "Everything about *Hamilton* took on a different tone today."

That performance would later lead to some speculation that Miranda had a bit of a shyness issue when it came to performing in front of celebrities, as witness the fact that the night Oprah Winfrey came to a performance, Miranda was also not scheduled to perform. Ahmir 'Questlove' Thompson, a member of the influential band The Roots and the producer of both the *Hamilton Original Cast Recording* and *The Hamilton Mixtape*, had a front row seat to Miranda's aversion to performing before high caliber celebrities and said as much to *Entertainment Weekly*. "Whenever a high profile celebrity would come, or someone of Obama's caliber, Lin would not do Hamilton."

Throughout the run of *Hamilton* on Broadway, Miranda was a dervish of creative motion. While maintaining the rigorous pace of *Hamilton* on a nightly basis and continuing to put the finishing touches on the music of *Moana*, he still found time to add a creative flourish to the Ham4Ham ticket lottery prior to each performance.

Twice a week, sometimes more, Miranda would appear outside where the lottery was about to be held, welcome the crowd and, as reported by *Slate,* would knock on the stage door and any number of performers

Marc Shapiro

would suddenly emerge and immediately launch into a mini performance that would often include Miranda. These performances were largely spontaneous creations of Miranda's, incorporating the skills of volunteer actors, dancers and singers in everything from poetry readings, improvisational rap comedy to an impromptu routine courtesy of The New York City Ballet. These performances, which included a rap duet inspired by *In the Heights* between Miranda and Jonathan Groff, a performance entitled *Hamilton's Cabinet Battle #1* and, as a Halloween treat, a new dance take on the song "Thriller."

Miranda felt the free performances were the least he could do as he explained to *Rolling Stone*. "I know that most of the hundreds of people who line up for the lottery won't win and I don't want them to walk away with nothing."

The lottery/free performances program would only last a few months before falling prey to complaints of traffic congestion, with the lottery reverting to online, a change that Miranda would often ease the guilt of diehard *Hamilton* fans freezing while waiting for their chance at tickets.

Even through its Broadway run, Miranda, ever the stickler for perfection was always on the lookout for ways to make *Hamilton* better. Which would often see him going underground in the theater to get a different perspective of a performance. And often in elaborate disguises to boot.

"Lin would rather watch them [the audience] than watch the show," Questlove related to *Entertainment Weekly*. "Lin sat in disguise. That's how much of a nerd and a dweeb Lin is."

Questlove could barely stifle the absurdity of Miranda's activity. As he would observe, Miranda was not only watching audience members but he was also mentally taking notes on how they were reacting to what was going on onstage. "He kept tabs on everyone who watched…who got the jokes, who laughed the most, who didn't get the jokes. He was like 'This one yawned at this part. This one was sleepy but I forgave them because I knew they were on a long flight. This one gave it three standing ovations.' "

Miranda, according to Questlove, often resorted to playing audience cop. There was the Obama day performance when Miranda jumped out of his seat in mid play and admonished the audience, good naturedly of course, for using their cell phones and taking selfies. There was even one very high profile celebrity, who was never admonished by name who was reportedly on the phone more than they were watching the play.

As it turned out, even a gentle soul like Miranda did have his breaking point. It was during the tail end of the Off Broadway production of *Hamilton* that Madonna made headlines for, reportedly, texting throughout the show. While not calling out Madonna by name, Miranda blasted a tweet that said, "Tonight was the first night that I asked stage management not to allow a celebrity {who was texting all through Act 2) backstage."

By August, Miranda had more on his plate than spying on audience members. Because of scheduling that had brought *Hamilton* to Broadway much sooner than expected, consequently there was now a sudden urgency in getting a *Hamilton Original Cast Recording* out. A deal had been struck with Atlantic Records to release the album and the label was expecting to hear something soon. But as the pressure built, Miranda was even more determined that the album should be done right and his way. He knew that most original cast albums were an afterthought, done on a budget, in a hurry and often unpolished, more as a souvenir to those who had seen a show than something that could stand on its own. Miranda would have none of that.

He wanted the *Hamilton Original Cast Recording* to have a vibrancy of sound and emotion that would easily rival the experience of seeing a live performance. To that end he brought in two members of his favorite group, Questlove and Black Thought, to produce. "That was my dream," declared Miranda to *Vanity Fair*. "The Roots played my Spring Fling senior year at Wesleyan College and I was a huge fan of The Roots' albums."

Avatar Studios would be booked for the sessions, staffed with top of the line engineers and a massive amount of recording equipment. Over a two week period in mid to late August, original cast members were shuttled in and out to recreate their live performances in the studio. The hoped for results were quickly evident as the performers did more than simply give a rote rendition of the *Hamilton* music, often lapsing into animated motion and emotion as they translated the vibe of their live performance into electrifying studio moments. Miranda's hopes that the album would resonate with people who had never seen a *Hamilton* performance was coming to fruition.

Hamilton Original Cast Recording had its digital release on September 25, 2015 and would be released in stores on October 16. The album was an immediate commercial success, debuting at No. 1 on the Top

Broadway Album Charts, No. 5 on the Top Digital Album Charts, #9 on the Top Current Album Charts and would peak at #1 on the Rap Album Charts and, in a nod to its hit status would peak at No. 3 on the Billboard Album Charts. The icing on the cake would be that the *Hamilton Original Cast* Album would chart in such international destinations as England, Ireland and Australia.

The massive success of *Hamilton* on Broadway, the success of the original cast album and, if the pundits were to be believed, the for certain boatload of Tony nominations looming in the coming year, had Miranda in the troughs of emotional turmoil. Personally and professionally, 2015 would be a year to savor for the rest of his life. Financially? It was a safe bet that Miranda and his family were not struggling. But in his most scattered moments, Miranda would tell the likes of *Billboard*, "I still live like a grad student."

In that same conversation with *Billboard*, Miranda allowed that, on occasion, his two perceptions of himself collided. "When The MacArthur Foundation called me, I picked up the phone thinking it was the cable company. I had just dumped them because their service sucked and I thought, 'This is probably them trying to get me back.' So I picked up the phone, real mad like 'What do you want? Your box breaks every 20 minutes.' I was crazy."

The response on the other end of the line would make him crazier. "This is Christina from The MacArthur Foundation"...

And she was informing Miranda that he had just won a $625,000 Genius grant.

Chapter Twenty-Four
I Thank You

On January 24, 2016, Miranda fulfilled a life long dream. It had nothing to do with *Hamilton*. For on that night, Miranda made an offstage cameo appearance as the Loud Hailer in the Broadway production of *Les Miserables*, thus fulfilling his lifelong ambition to appear in a production of the very first Broadway production he ever saw. With that dream fulfilled, Miranda could now get back to the business of being Miranda, which meant a lot to do on various fronts.

March 15, 2016 saw Miranda and members of the *Hamilton* cast return to The White House in a very charitable light, hosted performances, workshops, a Q&A session and a number of performances, the highlight for many being Miranda's performing a freestyle rap from prompts held up by President Obama. Obama said of that day, "We wanted to share this incredible musical with folks who might otherwise not have that experience."

April saw the publication of the book *Hamilton: The Revolution*. Co-authored by Miranda and Jeremy McCarter, the book chronicled the odyssey of *Hamilton* from conception to Broadway. *Hamilton: The Revolution* was an immediate success, selling out its entire first printing in short order and requiring the publisher to rush release a second printing to keep up with demand.

Now some months into 2016, *Hamilton* remained the star attraction despite the fact that Broadway, *Hamilton* aside, was having a banner year with a wide array of innovative productions, ethnically diverse casts and quite a number of musicals. Many critics were speculating that the rise to prominence of *Hamilton* was suddenly paving the way for the, of late, normally tradition bound/safe productions to take a few chances. Which made the upcoming awards season particularly promising.

An early indication that *Hamilton* was the odds on favorite to win everything in sight had already happened in February when *Hamilton* captured the Grammy for Best Theater Recording. Adding a bit of theatrical to the proceedings, *Hamilton* was right in the middle of a scheduled performance when the announcement was made and, with the world watching, Miranda happily stood at stage center with the rest of the cast, hoisting the Grammy award high and shouting "This is crazy! This is for you mom!"

April saw *Hamilton* gather that true rarity, a Pulitzer Prize for Best Drama, beating out two equally potent candidates, *Gloria* and *The Humans*. Miranda was exultant at the honor as reported by *Playbill*, when he acknowledged, "It's a tremendous honor to even be considered for this very prestigious award. To win today is beyond my wildest dreams."

It was a good thing Miranda made his living with words for, by May 2016 with the announcement of the Tony Awards nominees, he would need to summon up even more thanks as *Hamilton* would make Tony history with 16 nominations, more than any other show in Broadway history. The nominations in the categories of acting, writing, directing, dance, music and design quite literally left Miranda speechless. As reported by *The New York Times*, he managed, "It's unbelievable! It's absolutely humbling and incredible!"

Tony Awards night at The New York Beacon Theater was shaping up to be a joyous celebration for everyone connected with everybody's favorite show. Miranda was walking around in an excited daze, a grin from ear to ear was most certainly on his face as he contemplated the possibility of winning the biggest prize of all, Best Musical. Sadly, the vibe of the night was tempered when, at approximately 2:00 a.m., a lone gunman shot up gay night club Pulse killing and injuring countless club goers. Several hours later, as the theater community prepared to honor its own, there were serious questions about how to present the ceremony. What emerged was a somewhat somber, somewhat joyous celebration of the best that Broadway had to offer that, in speeches and in song, reached out to the world for peace, love and understanding. In its finest, often uplifting and inspiring moments, *Hamilton* would ultimately triumph with 11 Tony Awards that included Best Book of a Musical, Original Score, Lead Actor in a Musical (Leslie Odom Jr.), Featured Actor in a Musical (Daveed Diggs), Featured Actress in a Musical (Renee Elise Goldsberry), Costume Design (Paul Tazwell), Lighting Design (Howell Binkley), Director (Thomas Kail), Choreography (Andy Blankenbuhler) and Orchestration (Alex Lacamoire).

As the proceedings drew to a close, The Beacon Theater was alive with anticipation. Legendary singer/actress Barbara Streisand stepped to the podium and counted down the finalists for Best Musical. Somewhere in the audience, Miranda smiled a nervous smile and held his breath. Streisand opened the envelope and announced *Hamilton* as Best Musical. And the crowd went wild. Everybody in the house seemingly rose to their feet in unison and applauded and high fived a visibly overwhelmed Miranda as he made his way to the stage. His acceptance speech thanked everyone involved in the production, his family, his parents and ended with a heartfelt plea for peace and love.

Then it was time to party the night away.

Later in the evening, Miranda posted a selfie to the world. Miranda, most certainly overcome with emotion, appeared to be fast asleep, his head on the shoulder of his mother, a beatific smile on his face. In every possible way, Miranda was the toast of Broadway. But, at that moment, all he could think of to post under the selfie was...

"My mom y'all! It's been a bit of a day."

Chapter Twenty-Five
Hair Today Gone Tomorrow

July 9, 2016. It was the final performance of *Hamilton* with Miranda in the title role. For Miranda, it was a truly emotional and, by degrees, a freeing moment as he stood before an enthusiastic audience, taking his final bow of *Hamilton's* Broadway run. Moments after the final curtain came down, Miranda was backstage, scissors in hand, cutting off his long hair

It was a symbolic gesture to be sure. The length of Miranda's hair had mirrored the odyssey of *Hamilton* from conception to Broadway and his cutting of his locks mirrored, to a large extent, the end of one era and the beginning of another. Miranda took a single lock of shorn hair and photographed it against the backdrop of a white table and posted it on Twitter with the caption "Teach 'em how to say goodbye." Before going off to the after party in celebration of his final performance.

It all appeared pretty final. But following his triumph at the Tony Awards, Miranda, as reported by *People* and numerous other outlets, indicated that was not necessarily the case. "I have written a role I can't age out of. I intend to drop in on this over and over again. Cut to 20 years from now and you'll be like 'Lin, when will you stop playing Hamilton?' "

But Miranda could not completely cut even temporary ties with *Hamilton* until he kept his promise that there would be the long promised notion that started it all, *The Hamilton Mixtape*. It was a project that finally began to jell midway through 2016 and to say that it was ambitious was an understatement.

This 23 track album of covers and wildly divergent reinterpretations was an immediate and truly massive undertaking that corralled an all star team of artists and producers that included Alicia Keyes, The Roots, Regina Spektor, Ben Folds, Ashanti, Ja Rule, Johnny Legend, Usher, Common, Chance The Rapper and Miranda. The finished product would be a true confluence of influences and styles and would effectively open up the already progressive music of *Hamilton* to further possibilities. The album was released on December 2, 2016 and debuted at No. 1 on Billboard's Top 200 Chart, selling 187,000 copies right out of the box

Although he would manage to squeeze in bits and pieces of quiet time, which he would refer to as "vacation time and I really needed it," Miranda would have little time to contemplate the past. His notoriety had, not unexpectedly, brought him a flood of new opportunities. With its November 2016 release now set in stone, Miranda would continue to work on *Moana*. But of more personal importance, Miranda was doing his best to remember the Orlando nightclub shooting victims with a new charity single, recorded with superstar performer Jennifer Lopez, entitled "Love Make The World Go Round." The song, recorded over the July 4 holiday, sampled some of Miranda's Tony Awards acceptance speech. Miranda would also rap over the bridge of the song, a sample of which is "What we've got is love, even when the sinners hate us. We cannot let them diminish or intimidate us. We sing out."

Miranda could not completely leave his television acting behind, especially when it had to do with the reigning comic master Larry David and his show *Curb Your Enthusiasm*. Late in 2017, the opportunity to guest in a two-episode arc involving Larry writing *Fatwa: The Musical* with Miranda and attempting to get a ticket to *Hamilton* proved the ideal opportunity. Playing himself as a comedic straight man indicated that the composer/actor was doing more than moonlighting and that acting had become a solid component of who he wanted to be.

During this period, Miranda's political and social activism was also on display. Especially as it pertained to his native Puerto Rico issues. In March 2016, he returned to The White House, ostensibly to provide a day of workshops and song to invited guests but he also found time, along with a number of Democratic Senators including Kristen Gillibrand, Charles Schumer and Elizabeth Warren to voice his opinion on a call for Congressional action to back a bill that would allow Puerto Rico to declare bankruptcy and to ease its $70 billion tax burden, brought on by a slumping economy and a lack of jobs. Addressing reporters, Miranda stated, quite simply, that this is a fixable issue."

When it came to Puerto Rico, Miranda, almost immediately, found himself at odds with newly minted US President Donald Trump due to his travel ban and anti-immigrant policies and declarations. Miranda was often a commanding presence at street protests and was not afraid to go on the attack when he thought Trump was off base on an issue. Which was very much the case in 2017 when hurricane relief in Puerto Rico was spotty at best and, largely, the result of blatant neglect by The White House. Trump, as he was prone to do, took any attacks personally and was quick to respond with bullying tweets, which was the case when the President accused the Mayor of San Juan of "poor leadership" in response to her pleas for aid for hurricane victims. Miranda was upset by the uncaring attitude projected by Trump and, as reported by *The Washington Examiner* and other media outlets, blasted out a tweet of his own directed at the President. "You're going straight to hell. No lines for you. Right this way sir. They'll clear a path."

Miranda's work on *Moana*, which to this day he credits with keeping his head on straight, succeeded in putting him on 'The Mouse Factory's' radar for a couple of upcoming projects. A reported live action remake of *The Little Mermaid* struck at nostalgia but Miranda had not completely settled on the project in a conversation with *The New York Times*. "I know that's been out there but its super early. We haven't formalized anything. I would say I'm invested emotionally but not attached."

A Disney project that definitely had his attention was a long talked about sequel entitled *Mary Poppins Returns*. Miranda had actually been officially cast in late February 2016 with the idea that his first major motion picture acting job, opposite Emily Blunt, would also entail him writing much of the soundtrack.

At the time of a conversation with *Cinema*

Blend.com, Miranda was still some months away from beginning filming but seemed enthusiastic about the prospects of his role of Jack the street lamplighter. "This takes place about 20 years after the original Mary Poppins film. But I get to be around for the adventures of Mary and the kids and sing and dance and do all the fun things."

Almost after the fact, Miranda has offered that once *Mary Poppins Returns* reportedly begins filming, he will be looking at a window of approximately six months when the only thoughts he will be entertaining will be non-*Hamilton* in nature. But during the months following his last *Hamilton* appearance, he was finding time to unwind and relax and contemplate the up and down sides of his sudden celebrity. Thanks, in large part, to a media that simply would not let any aspect of Miranda's life in the spotlight go. Sure *Hamilton* was, for the time being, over for him. But the questions, supplied by a never-ending rush of media that included the likes of *Variety, G*Q and *Rolling Stone* wanted more and, although Miranda was often described as visibly wrung out, he remained ever accommodating and candid in looking back.

He acknowledges the irony that as *Hamilton* grew in popularity, he had to modify how he dealt with people. Fans were camping out all night in the hopes of getting tickets. literal mosh pits began to greet him as he made his way in and out of the theater. "I started to get very nervous about approaching the theater and leaving the theater. It got to the point where I couldn't sign autographs at the stage door. That was painful. The secret exits in and out of the theater got to be very tough to deal with."

Miranda compared the latter stages of his Broadway experience with his time Off Broadway, longing for the latter. The growing mania for all things *Hamilton* and, by association, himself were palpable in his memories. "Outside the theater I had some safety concerns. Because of my concerns for people standing near the barriers. I just had to stop at a certain point because I felt it wasn't safe for them."

There were also moments, near the end of his Broadway run, where he often feared for his own safety. A new brand of professional autograph hunters had begun to invade his world, the ones who get autographs and then turn around and sell them. And as Miranda recalled, they could be extremely aggressive in pursuit of his signature. "There were times when they would chase my car all the way down Sixth Avenue and every time we would stop at a light they would start banging on the car windows, surrounding the car."

Miranda is well aware that he is paying a price for celebrity that most people would sell their soul to have. But Miranda, by nature, has always been a real world person who likes to move through his life in some semblance of anonymity. And he is philosophical and, to a degree, saddened by the notion that the very thing that he sought has somehow taken away what he had.

"When I wake up in the morning, I feel the same," he maintains. "But when I leave the house that's the measure of how different the world is, coming out here and being a selfie magnet in the streets of New York City."

Miranda is steadfast in his hopes that post *Hamilton* he can return to some semblance of normal life. "I still want to live in the world." But he admits that even the simplest of pleasures, walking down the street or riding the train, have been severely compromised. "You choose your level of involvement with the world on the train. You can talk to your neighbor or you can be in your cocoon. I like being able to choose my engagement with the world. When *Hamilton* was at its peak, and I couldn't ride the train without people wanting to talk to me the entire train ride, that was tough because I no longer had the choice of engagement. I hope to get it back one day."

But it is the non-stop thought and creativity that continues to drive him that will seemingly forever keep him in the spotlight. Post *Hamilton*, he admits to a number of ideas "that I carry around with me like luggage," giving only vague notions rather than specifics. "I think some of them might be movies and some of them might be the germ of a TV series. One of them might be a stage show."

All of which will, most certainly, add to a legacy of accomplishment that many consider set in stone for the ages. Not surprisingly, Miranda tends to look at what his legacy might be in less lofty terms. "If I have a good idea and I don't live to see it out, then there it goes. That's it. I had an early sense of mortality. So getting as much stuff done before you're dead is a huge motivating factor for me. I've always approached my life and work thinking, 'How much can I get away with doing before I go?'"

Chapter Twenty-Six
Money for Something

Growing up, Miranda and the concept of a lot of money were often at odds. Either he did not have much or when he did, he did not know how to handle it.

"There is so much I wish I knew about money when I was first starting out my adult life," he confessed during a conversation with the website *Morgan Stanley.com*. "Growing up, I was always cautious about spending. I was so nervous about incurring debt that I didn't open my first credit card until I was 28, after my first show had opened on Broadway. Even though I had enough money in the bank, I didn't have sufficient credit history to purchase my first apartment. My father had to help me to buy it by co-signing the mortgage."

But that was then. While he acknowledges that he was financially comfortable with the success of *In the Heights*, it would take *Hamilton* to put the young composer on easy street. And we know that because the dollars and cents of Miranda's bank balance are out there for the public to see. While what people in 'the business' make has always been, by design, a deep dark secret, usually known only to managers, agents and spouses, in the case of Miranda, there has been a surprising degree of transparency in which the likes of *Morgan Stanley.com, The New York Times, Fortune, The Hollywood Reporter* and *Business Insider* have gone public with the facts and figures of Miranda's money business.

For openers, Miranda reportedly made $6.4 million during the first year of *Hamilton's* Broadway run. This breaks down as follows: He receives weekly royalties which include seven percent of the show's weekly box office gross of an estimated $105,000 (based on an estimated $1.5 million weekly gross. Miranda was also due another three percent in royalties of the show's net profit after the show's investors recouped their reported initial $12.5 million investment, which, according to all reports, happened shortly after Hamilton's debut on Broadway.

And when it comes to Miranda's creative rights surrounding Hamilton…well he basically owns them all. Miranda came up with the idea for *Hamilton*, wrote the music, the lyrics and the book, for which he receives royalties. Said creative royalties also extend to other media, including royalties from sales of the *Hamilton Original Cast Recording, The Hamilton Mixtape* and, as an author, royalties from the sales of the book *Hamilton: The Revolution*.

Following the money trail also leads to the myriad of licensed merchandise, everything from T-shirts to programs, to coffee mugs and all items in between. And as long as a production of *Hamilton* is held anywhere in the world post Broadway, Miranda will be getting a generous share of the performing rights. And lest we forget, Miranda continues to draw royalties from *In the Heights* and will be making newfound money with the success of *Moana* and his contribution to *Star Wars: The Force Awakens*.

That he was materially set for life was almost an afterthought for Miranda. At the end of the day the most important thing about having the money was that it gave him the freedom to do whatever he wanted to do.

Chapter Twenty-Seven
What Dreams May Come

When Miranda and his wife Vanessa were photographed walking down the red carpet during the December 2017 London Evening Standard Theater Awards, one thing was very obvious. And that was that Vanessa was very pregnant.

Miranda would finally confirm that his wife and he were expecting their second child in an enthusiastic tweet "Oh hell yeah." He would further acknowledge that it had long been a happily well-kept secret in the Miranda family and that even their now two-year-old son Sebastian was in on the secret as tweeted by Miranda "He [Sebastian] is so impatient for it. Sebastian wants to know when mommy is gonna hatch?"

It would be a New Years gift indicative of the good cheer and prosperity that would follow Miranda into 2018. There was already talk of a Grammy nomination for his work on *Moana* in his immediate future. And while he was, for the time being, finished with acting in *Hamilton*. His dealing with his creation was far from over. While in the UK working in front of the camera on *Mary Poppins Returns,* behind the scenes Miranda was actively involved in the casting of the London production of *Hamilton*. He was also monitoring the progress of the national tour of *Hamilton*.

The big question in bringing *Hamilton* across the pond to London's famed West End was how well the decidedly American creation would play in the UK. Miranda had already had an idea that his creations might be universal back in 2011 when a London production of *In the Heights* did quite well with foreign audiences. But the ever-confident Miranda conceded that *Hamilton* overseas might take a bit of doing. The bottom line being would anybody outside of America really care? Then there was the fact that the only British character in the musical, George III, is portrayed, according to Miranda "as a flamboyant fob" which might rub audiences the wrong way. But Miranda was not deterred as he went about the process of assembling a British cast. "It's a similar mix of vets and newcomers as we had in the original company on Broadway," he remarked to BBC News. Miranda was encouraged at *Hamilton's* overseas prospects when no lesser light than actress Helen Mirren told him that the show would do just fine in the UK.

But it would take the first run through with the British cast to convince the composer that he had nothing to worry about. "London, gird your heart," he tweeted. "This company is not playing around. This company is so fucking good!"

Ever the perfectionist, Miranda still had second thoughts and would ultimately tweak the lyrics of three *Hamilton* songs to better accommodate the British sensibilities. For the song "Take a Break," which originally had Hamilton saying, "John Adams

167

doesn't have a real job anyway." Miranda replaced the line with "Vice President isn't a real job anyway." In "Your Obedient Servant," which originally contained the line "They should meet in Weehawken," was replaced with the single word "Jersey." Finally the song "The Room Where It Happens" and its line, "Well, I propose The Potomac" was changed to "We'll have him over, propose it."

Ultimately *Hamilton* mania travelled quite well with a successful run and good notices. Then it was back to the States where a national tour of *Hamilton* continued to fan the flames of interest and hype which, in turn, was offering Miranda even further creative options.

With the buzz centering around his work on *Moana*, the rest of the world was beating a path to Miranda's door. Lionsgate was early in the race to ink Miranda's services when they signed the composer as executive producer on a projected film, television series and, possible, stage adaptation based on the series of fantasy/magic/music novels of Patrick Rothfuss entitled *The Kingkiller Chronicles*. Miranda tweeted to confirm this seemingly massive undertaking. "I love the world of Patrick Rothfuss and I want to spend time figuring out how to share this with you. So this is happening."

Also on the horizon from Sony is a deal in which Miranda would produce 11 songs to be used in the upcoming animated film *Vivo*, the story of a monkey with a thirst for adventure. And the twists and turns of Miranda's involvement in the live action version of Disney's *The Little Mermaid* seemed to be rounding into shape when *Deadline.com* and several other outlets reported that Miranda would be paired with legendary composer Alan Menken to create the music for the film.

Less clear were the never-ending stories speculating on film adaptations of both *Hamilton* and *In the Heights*. To those, Miranda would only concede that he would be interested in both projects getting a film treatment but nothing was set in stone at this point. But one thing was certain, into January 2018, Miranda had truly arrived at the end of a magic odyssey, one born of hard work, passion and persistence, one that had literally become a real life mirror of the fantasy worlds he has created.

And one that leaves him on the cusp of whatever comes next. Which, of late, has seen the mercurial Miranda respond to questions of creative mortality much like a wise old philosopher rather than a creative genius who is still a couple of years away from touching 40.

There is a new life entering his world and, with it, more responsibility to consider and ultimately deal with. There are the ideals of being a good husband, father and son, the traditional aspects of his nature, which he is anxious to add the next chapter to. And finally, and this is where Miranda feels luckier than most, that he can continue to make a satisfying life for himself doing what he loves most.

"One thing I can say for certain is that you will not see another American history musical from me," he told *CNBC*. "I've done that about as well as I think I can do it. So I'll write something else. I'm excited to see what that will be."

In examining the life and times of Lin-Manuel

Miranda, one element of his life and career keeps popping up. And that is what is certain the relative ease in Miranda's psyche, now that he has entered a period of relative calm in his life, he is determined not to become a 'one hit wonder' who will knock himself out to top himself at whatever cost. "I'm trying to get out of the 'this tops that' way of thinking. That way lies madness. All I can control is what I make. The world will do with it what it will."

But Miranda is finally well aware that whatever his future holds for him, it will be the same process that brought *Hamilton* and *In The Light* into his life and made him a true life success story. "The work will be hard," he offered in a tweet. "But it will be worth it."

Chapter Twenty-Eight
History in the Making

With the Tony Awards already being seen as the ultimate validation of *Hamilton's* success, to Miranda's way of thinking there were literally no more worlds to conquer and accolades to contemplate. But that thinking changed on April 18, 2016 when The Pulitzer Prize committee announced that *Hamilton* had won the prestigious award for Best Drama, a truly prestigious award that had been given out to the best theater had to offer since 1917.

Miranda was truly speechless at the news. But not for long.

"It's a tremendous honor to even be considered for this prestigious award," he excitedly related to *Playbill.com*. "Quiara (*Hamilton* writer Quiara Alegria Hurdes) and I were elated to have been recognized as finalists for *In the Heights* (nominated for a Pulitzer nomination in 2009). So to win for *Hamilton* is beyond my wildest dreams. This award is for everyone who has been a part of this six-plus years' journey."

Equally impressive in Hamilton's Pulitzer win was that it became only the ninth musical in the 100-year history of the award to capture top honors, joining the ranks of previous winners *Of Thee I Sing, South*

Pacific, *Fiorello!*, *How To Succeed In Business Without Really Trying*, *A Chorus Line*, *Sunday In The Park With George*, *Rent* and *Next To Normal*. It was a moment that Miranda noted in his conversation with *Playbill.com*.

"To be the ninth musical to ever win The Pulitzer Prize for drama in its 100 year history is truly humbling for all of us and is simply outside our comprehension. Look at where we are! Look at where we started."

Miranda's Pulitzer triumph would usher in a rush of many and varied honors over the next two years. Two thousand seventeen saw Miranda nominated for an Emmy for Outstanding Guest Actor in a Comedy Series for his appearance on *Saturday Night Live* while The Producer's Guild of America would nominate Miranda for Outstanding Producer of Non Fiction Television for the documentary *Hamilton's America*.

The success of the animated film *Moana* would pave the way for Miranda in the 2017 Golden Globes and Academy Awards nominations for Best Original Song for "How Far I'll Go." By 2018, Miranda would also be mining Grammy gold, capturing honors for Best Song Written for Visual Media for "How Far I'll Go" and a nomination for Best Compilation Soundtrack For Visual Media.

Even the lesser known but equally prestigious Laurence Olivier Awards, named for the legendary actor to honor outstanding creative achievement, which saw fit, in 2018, to honor Miranda and *Hamilton* for Outstanding Achievement In Music. Needless to say, the joke going around the theater community was that Miranda was rapidly running out of space on his mantle for all the hardware honoring his creativity.

Miranda's notoriety had made him the toast of the town, especially when it came to stepping out at different events with a social and political stance. There was seemingly a situation that Miranda could rarely saw no to. In a sense, he saw it as his way of giving back and that's why the composer always seemed to have an event on his plate. There was the spirited and revealing interview at the Anthony Quinn Foundation, the thunderous applause that greeted The President's Merit Award at The Latin Grammys and his tour of The White House halls that helped inspire *Hamilton* on route to accepting The Capital Historical Society's Freedom Award.

But, inevitably, Miranda's thoughts would keep returning to The Pulitzer Prize which, if perception counted for anything, was running neck and neck with The Tony Awards in Miranda's list of accomplishments. When The Pulitzer Prize judges couched their announcement with "*Hamilton* is a landmark American musical," Miranda's legacy seemed assured.

But on the day of the announcement, Miranda was once again the excited creative mind that had entered the world of theater on a wing and a prayer. He was tweeting up a storm.

But all that he could think of to say was "grateful, grateful, grateful" over and over again.

Appendix

Theater Credits
In the Heights
(1999-2010-2011)

Actor, composer and lyricist
West Side Story
(2009)
Spanish translations

Working
(2011)
Wrote two new songs

Merrily We Roll Along
(2012)
Actor

Bring It On: The Musical
(2012)
Co-composer and lyricist

21 Chump Street
(2014)
Actor, playwright, composer, lyricist

Tick...Tick...Boom
(2014)
Actor

Hamilton
(2015-2016)
Actor, playwright, composer, lyricist

Les Miserables
(2016)
Actor

Filmography

Film
Clayton's Friend
(1996)
Actor, writer, producer, director, editor

The Odd Life of Timothy Green
(1996)
Actor

The Polar Bears
(2012)
Actor

200 Cartas
(2013)
Actor

Star Wars: The Force Awakens
(2015)
Actor and special featured composer

Studio Heads
(2015)
Actor as himself

Moana
(2016)
Composer and singer

Hamilton's America
(2016)
Actor (himself)

Speech & Debate
(2017)
Actor

Mary Poppins Returns
(2018)
Actor

Television

The Sopranos
(2007)
Actor

Sesame Street
(2009-2012)
Actor, composer, lyricist

House
(2009)
Actor

The Electric Company
(2009-2010)
Actor and composer

Modern Family
(2009-2010)
Actor

Submissions Only
(2011)
Actor

Freestyle Love Supreme
(2012
Actor and lyricist

Do No Harm
(2012)
Actor

Smash
(2012)
Actor (himself)

How I Met Your Mother
(2013)
Actor

Bojack Horseman
(2016)
Actor

The Magic Schoolbus Rides Again
(2017)
Singer (theme song)

Curb Your Enthusiasm
(2017)
Actor

Duck Tales
(2018)
Actor (voice role)

Discography

Original Cast Albums
In the Heights
(2008)

21 Chump Street
(2014)
Hamilton
(2015)

The Hamilton Mixtape
(2017)

Sources

Interviews

I would like to thank Irv Steinfink for his time and memories.

Books

Hamilton: The Revolution by Jeremy McCarter and Lin-Manuel Miranda.

Magazines

Gentleman's Quarterly, Vogue, New York Lifestyle, The New Yorker, Vibe, Complex, NEA Magazine, AARP, Newsweek, Paste, Glamour, Rolling Stone, Billboard, Time Out New York, US Magazine, Entertainment Weekly, Vanity Fair, People, Fortune

Newspapers

The Guardian, Business Insider, The New York Times, Associated Press, Los Angeles Daily News, The Washington Post, Cleveland Plain Dealer, Variety, Orange County Register, Los Angeles Times, New York Post, The Hollywood Reporter, The Times, The Boston Globe,

Websites

My Heritage.com, GQ.com, Playbill.com, AMNY Network.com, Hispanic Scholarship.com, I Interview

Playwrites.com, WFMT.com, Grantland.com, Spokesman.com, Educational Theater Association.com, Kennedy Center.org, Chrishayes.org, Viceland.com, New York.com, Swarthmore.com, Broadway Backstory.com, Latina.com, Hesherman.com, Broadway Bullet.com, Broadway World.com, Theater Mania.com, Vulture.com, Vox.com, The Huffington Post.com, Smithsonian.com, Mental Floss.com, CNBC.com, Fast Company.com, The Junto.com, American Theater.com, Cinema Blend.com, Morgan Stanley.com, Deadline.com, Black Book.com, BBC News

Television
NBC news, 60 Minutes, Charlie Rose, MSNBC,

Radio
National Public Radio,

Miscellaneous
Megan Smolenyak blog entry, Broadway League speech, Extra Newsfeed blog, Lin-Manuel Miranda Twitter, blog and selfie entries, WTF podcast, In the Heights: Chasing Broadway Dreams (documentary), Wesleyan commencement speech, Broadway.com, Tony Awards acceptance speech, Tonight Show anecdotes,

Disaster Relief for Puerto Rico

Lin-Manuel Miranda's passion for aiding in the relief and recovery for Puerto Rico has manifested itself in a series of hats, shirts and other merchandise being sold through TeeRico.com with 100% of the proceeds from sales going to disaster relief. Those wishing to make a donation to Puerto Rico disaster relief can go to Unidos at https://www.unidosporpuertorico.com/en/

About the Author

New York Times bestselling author Marc Shapiro has written more than 60 nonfiction celebrity biographies, more than two-dozen comic books, numerous short stories and poetry, and three short form screenplays. He is also a veteran freelance entertainment journalist.

His young adult book *JK Rowling: The Wizard Behind Harry Potter* was on *The New York Times* bestseller list for four straight weeks. His fact-based book *Total Titanic* was also on *The Los Angeles Times* bestseller list for four weeks. *Justin Bieber: The Fever* was on the nationwide Canadian bestseller list for several weeks.

Shapiro has written books on such personalities as Shonda Rhimes, George Harrison, Carlos Santana, Annette Funicello, Lorde, Lindsay Johan, E.L. James, Jamie Dornan, Dakota Johnson, Adele and countless others. He also co-authored the autobiography of mixed martial arts fighter Tito Ortiz, *This Is Gonna Hurt: The Life of a Mixed Martial Arts Champion*.

He is currently working on a biography of Senator John McCain as well as updating his biographies of Gillian Anderson and Lucy Lawless for Riverdale Avenue Books.

Other Riverdale Avenue Books Titles by Marc Shapiro

You're Gonna Make It After All:
The Life, Times and Influence of Mary Tyler Moore

Hey Joe: The Unauthorized Biography of a Rock
Classic

Trump This! The Life and Times of Donald Trump,
An Unauthorized Biography

The Secret Life of EL James

The Real Steele: The Unauthorized Biography of
Dakota Johnson

Inside Grey's Anatomy: The Unauthorized
Biography of Jamie Dornan

Annette Funicello: America's Sweetheart

Game: The Resurrection of Tim Tebow

Legally Bieber: Justin Bieber at 18

Lindsay Lohan: Fully Loaded, From Disney to
Disaster

Printed in Great Britain
by Amazon